# THE ART
# OF . . .
# SUCCESS

# THE ART OF SUCCESS

BY

## T. SHARPER KNOWLSON

AUTHOR OF "THE ART OF THINKING"

"Nothing succeeds like Success"
*Talleyrand*

FREDERICK WARNE AND CO.
NEW YORK AND LONDON
1902

Press of J. J. Little & Co.
Astor Place, New York

TO
*MY WIFE*

# PREFACE

THERE are several accepted opinions as to the
kind of man who should undertake the writing
of a book on the principles of Success. It
is held by some that he should be a man of
wealth—wealth which he has earned by the
unaided use of his own powers. Others hold
that wealth is not a necessary qualification in
any sense; all that is needed is the ability to
observe life, and to draw correct inferences
from its phenomena. As to which of these
views may be correct, it is hardly my business
to say; and although every writer is expected
to consider his competency for the task essayed,
it frequently happens that his love for a subject
over-rides this very proper demand for suitable credentials. The very hearty reception
accorded to my previous little volume on " The
Art of Thinking " has led me to believe that a

similar book on Success would not be unacceptable. There is, of course, a vast difference between the abstract world of thought and the concrete world of action, and a man may be a skilful guide in one and at the same time a failure in the other. Still, life is a blend of thought and action, and in this sense " The Art of Success " is directly supplementary to " The Art of Thinking." And if a more than generous allowance be given to the results of observation and reflection, as expressed in plain English, I may then venture to offer the following pages in the hope that they may prove helpful and suggestive to those for whose benefit they were specially written.

# CONTENTS

## CHAPTER I

INTRODUCTION . . . . . pp. 1-5

## CHAPTER II

### SUCCESS: SOME ATTEMPTS AT A DEFINITION

Success, ideal and real—Pills and poems—Success in finance and medicine—A *man* v. *a machine*—One point of view stated . . . . . . . pp. 6-15

## CHAPTER III

### IS SUCCESS INCREASINGLY DIFFICULT?

Yes and No—Competition—Incompetency—Vacancies for the competent—Larger salaries to fewer men—Need of capital—Trusts—Success and past achievements—No finality in business—The difficult not impossible
pp. 16-33

## CHAPTER IV

### LUCK? OR NO LUCK?

The word as commonly used—Luck and Nature—Luck and a voyage—Luck and geology—Luck on the Stock Exchange—Luck and civilisation—Luck in opportunities—Success independent of luck—The real unlucky man—Theory of luck stated—Luck and foresight—Fatalism . . . . . . . pp. 34-51

## CHAPTER V

## THE HANDICAP OF LIMITATIONS

Rose-water optimism—Easy recipes for success—No success tabloid—Physical limitations—Mental—Moral—The best brains win, but character is chiefest—Lack of interest a vice of character—Some businesses more profitable than others—The salaried man—The curse of sport

pp. 52–69

## CHAPTER VI

## WHAT IS YOUR WORK?

The misery of the misfits—Finding the right place—Parental vanities—Trades *v.* professions—Know yourself and trust yourself—Self-knowledge and self-realisation

pp. 70–77

## CHAPTER VII

## ORIGINALITY: THE KEY

Originality defined—In literature and in business—The thinker always leads—Can originality be developed ?— Men of one idea—The key to success, and why—New businesses pay best . . . . pp. 78–85

## CHAPTER VIII

## HOW SOME MEN HAVE SUCCEEDED

Success biography—Its continuity—Sir W. P. Treloar—Sir R. Tangye—Walter Hazell, M.P.—J. M. Richards—Sir George Newnes, Bart.—Evan Spicer—Sir P. Manfield —C. Moberly Bell—Sir Wm. Dunn—Sir James Reckitt Sir T. J. Lipton, Bart.—J. S. Fry—T. H. W. Idris— C. A. Pearson—Thomas Smith—The moving power is vital interest . . . . . pp. 86–100

# CONTENTS

Influence and success—Education and success—Capital and
success—The use of business maxims—Why deserving
men fail . . . . . . pp. 101-117

Be practical—The power of initiative—The manipulation
of business figures—Be a specialist—The duty of the
salaried man—Cultivate a sense of humour—The value
of tact . . . . . . pp. 118-154

CONCLUSION . . . . . pp. 155-163

# THE ART OF SUCCESS

## CHAPTER I

### INTRODUCTION

*"To wish is of slight moment; thou oughtest to desire with earnestness to be successful."*—OVID.

THE subject of success is as old as the hills, but it is one of perennial interest; and the difficulty presented to the writer is not that of a lack of materials, but of the capacity to select from a mountain heap those facts and principles which are fundamental, together with the truths that directly express the spirit of the age. Whether or not the chapters that follow are instances of happy selection and expression must be left to the judgment of the reader; suffice it for the present if we give an outline of our object, and the methods employed to accomplish it.

1. We aim at telling *the real truth about success*. The implication is, of course, that it is usually obscured. This is true. Actuated by a laudable purpose to inspire hopefulness of outlook and endeavour, men have written and spoken as if the difference between man and man had little effect on the struggle for position: any man who set his heart on a great achievement could, and would, be victorious. The dangers of pessimism are many, but there are dangers in optimism too, and these ought to be pointed out, even though it is best to " err in the right direction." Our policy is to be true to facts, irrespective of their influences upon mind and feeling; but we shall prove conclusively that for most people the world is rather hope‑full than hope‑less.

There is another reason why the real truth about success needs to be told: it is because there are already so many " keys " and " secrets,"—the result being that the keys do not all of them fit, and the secrets do not reveal. For instance, one writer will say, " Religion is the key to success." We have so much respect for true religion that we do not care to be rude to him and say, " It is not." At the same time we can think of some who, though " they walked in white," and were saints in deed and of a truth, could never keep business going without a subsidy. That religion may contribute certain elements of strength no one will deny; but, taken by itself, it is neither the true key nor the real secret. The same remarks apply to claims set up in favour of total abstinence, punctuality, early rising, economy, and many other virtues. The secret of success is not a single element, but a compound of a selected group; and although vital interest is the power which fuses them together, it is not of itself alone sufficient to accomplish the desired end: there must be intelligent guidance.

2. As to the methods we shall employ, the first duty lies in defining success by analysing the word in its accepted meaning, and its application to various types of successful life. It will be seen that there is success of fine quality where dollars are fewest; but as this represents idealism, and our immediate purpose is achievement on the plane of the real, we shall limit ourselves to business success

by business methods, leaving the principles of higher life out of our purview altogether.

Difficulties are next considered. Reasons will be given for saying that success becomes increasingly difficult, and the subject of luck receives systematic treatment. Limitations of all kinds are then discussed: physical, mental, and moral. Frank admissions are made on this topic of disabilities, but the positive side is not neglected; indeed, we show that difficulties, though an increasing quantity, are not necessarily impossibilities; that luck is frequently another name for cunning foresight; and that character is often responsible for greater achievements than powers of mind.

We shall next deal with the more constructive side of success, the first point being the emphatic need of finding a suitable occupation. Using the word " key " in its correct manner, we claim that originality is the key that opens the door of notable prosperity. After defining originality in its relation to commerce, an object lesson is provided in chapter viii., " How Some Men Have Succeeded." The selection of men is modern, having regard to present conditions, and the need of a variation from

types of a past century. Such points as do
not directly arise out of the subject in its
chapter divisions are dealt with in " Questions
and Answers," and a series of " Practical
Counsels " brings the volume to a conclusion.
It will be a pleasure to us if the reader's final
impression—in spite of plain speaking—is one
of hope and determination.

# CHAPTER II

## SUCCESS: SOME ATTEMPTS AT A
## DEFINITION

*" The only failure a man ought to fear
is failure in cleaving to the purpose he
sees to be best."*—George Eliot.

WHEN Socrates heard the Athenians speak
of justice and virtue, he was accustomed to ask
them what they meant by these words; and,
as often as not, failed to obtain a satisfactory
reply. He was calling philosophy down

**Socrates on definitions.** from heaven by the simple expedient
of demanding an occasional definition; and at
the same time he was calling down on his own
head the hearty dislike of people who resent
inconvenient questions. In fact, the death of
Socrates has been ascribed to his crime in
saying *ad nauseam*, " What do you mean? "
The offence seems hardly serious enough for
a cup of hemlock, but there is no doubt that

6

Socrates was a most annoying person in conversation, with his everlasting "Define! Define!"

And yet we must have definitions. The first requisite of an intelligent interchange of opinions is that the words shall, as nearly as possible, possess the same meaning in every speaker's mouth; otherwise the talk degenerates into confusion, and too often into undignified vexation of spirit. Take the word *success*. We open a dictionary and read, "a favourable or prosperous termination **Success** of anything attempted." That is both **defined.** simple and comprehensive, for it includes everything, from the polishing of a pair of boots to the formation of a Billion Dollar Trust.

But this is not what men have in their minds when they talk about success. As a rule they mean money. A Senior Wrangler is not thought of as a successful man; he is allowed to be *brilliant* and *distinguished,* but he is not the equal, so far as success is concerned, of the egg and butter merchant who has made his pile, bought a street of houses, and retired into comfortable obscurity. Yes; success connotes something tangible in its

everyday meaning—something on the lines
of realism; whilst the scholar, and all who
contribute to the ideal, are sharply marked off
under another heading; they are "distinguished." But if the lexicographer is correct, a man may be successful even though
he does nothing more to earn the title
than the writing of a dozen brilliant
essays; and if success is the prosperous
termination of *anything* attempted, then those
who by circumstances are compelled to be
hewers of wood and drawers of water, can,
if they work well, claim to be successful
men, though not "distinguished." Whatever elements there are in success as a
modern phenomenon, the commercial is by
far the most preponderant. Let us suppose
we have two men before us: a pharmacist
who has created a new pill, and a poet who
has created a new poem. It may be a moot
question as to which of these men will render
the greater service to the community, but
for our purposes it will be sufficient to pre-
sume that the pill and the poem are respec-
tively adapted to the needs of the body and
the mind. What is to be done to make a

Success: ideal and real.

success of them? Put them on the market and advertise them freely: the pill to be accompanied by striking testimonials, and **Pills and** the poem by snippets from the best **poems.** reviews. Granting a measure of comparative merit to both articles, the final result will soon be apparent. The poet will get a fair amount of fame, but not much money; the pharmacist will gather in the shekels rapidly and care nothing about the fame. To begin with, the pill has a better chance than the poem; so strange is the idiosyncrasy of the public that it is satisfied with a few thousand copies of the latter, whilst it goes on buying the former as long as the proprietor chooses to advertise. Again, the public is not interested in the pharmacist as a man, except, perhaps, in the spirit of passing curiosity; but it rather reveres the name of the poet, and, when he is dead, is prepared to pay more for his pen-wiper than for a volume of his poems.

After all, both these men succeeded—one in the Ideal, and the other in the Real, the only difference being that the monetary rewards of ideal contributions to the world's wealth are seldom so large as those which arise out of industry on the plane of the real. *Paradise Lost* did not fetch a big price in the currency of the day, but in striving to obtain a true idea of successful life we ought to remember that soul-supremacy of Milton's type is a more significant thing for history than the piling up of material riches; and yet material riches are to most people synonymous with success.

Up to the present we have said little about the subject in its relation to the *man*. As before, we will choose two as representing very different spheres of occupation: a country doctor and a great financier. The doctor has four affections: nature, literature, humanity, and medicine. The woods and hills and meadows are a perpetual feast to his eye and imagination; he revels in books, and handles them in the delicate manner of one to whom they are as real as friends; he is beloved by the people for his self-sacrificing kindness and devotion; and he spares no expense in keeping himself abreast of the times in medical knowledge in order that his people may have the best of advice and skill. When the end comes he leaves a very moderate fortune and a name which travels no farther,

Success in finance and medicine.

perhaps, than the boundaries of the county in which he lived. Now look at the financier. He has only *one* affection: money. There is nothing about money he does not know. You cannot surprise him in a matter of finance: stocks, shares, prices this year, prices last year, prices ten years ago—he knows these things as well as we know the multiplication table. But this money-affection has serious disadvantages. It turns everything to gold, and nothing could be worse than that. The beauty of an idea is lost sight of altogether; in fact, the only beautiful ideas are those with money in them. The financier's library must be an interesting study in metallic selection: the *Il Penseroso* is not in the running with a mining report. And when the end comes, what then? A huge fortune left behind— nothing more. Jay Gould once said: **Jay Gould.** "I cannot remember ever to have had a good turn done to me. I am not surprised, for I have had to shove down every man I ever met. I have made my own fortune, and in doing so I have had to ruin thousands." One would like to know how far these words are penitential, or how far they express the self-satisfaction of a man who has fought and won.

In comparing the country doctor with the great financier, we see at a glance that the former was a *man,* the latter a money-making *machine;* the man of medicine realised *himself,* the man of money realised a *fortune.* There is no mawkish sentiment or empty moralising about these statements; all country doctors are not saints, and all great financiers are not sinners; it is no more a crime to make money by money than it is to do so by healing diseases or setting broken bones. The real point is this: the life of one was true to human perspective, the life of the other was—distortion.  To be just, we must admit that even distortion may be impressive, and the history of Jay Gould's millions is not destitute of facts which appeal to the emotions of courage and endurance; but at the last it declares itself a fantastic failure—an avenue of glittering gold, unrelieved by a touch of nature or a ray of spiritual light.

True to human perspective!  The doctor

**A man** *versus* **a machine.**

was a *man;* his was no starved soul that saw
only money in his patients' aches and pains,
nor did he look on the woods with a single
eye to the timber market, or on the broad
acres with a view to building schemes. Rather
than " shove " men down he tried to help
them up.

Which of these two was the more successful man? In the commercial sense, the
financier; in the ideal sense, the doctor.
Thus it is possible for a man to achieve
great worldly prosperity, and yet fail ignomini-
ously from the human point of view; he becomes a piece of mechanism for grinding out
dollars. On the other hand, ideal success
consists of self-realisation—the symmetrical
development of physical, mental, moral, and
social powers. Of course there are men who
succeed commercially and in every other way;
others succeed in every other way but not
commercially; others again do not succeed
at all.

In these pages the prevailing conception will
be business success. We are not taking high
ground simply because the demand upon space
and on adequacy of treatment is too great; so

**Success:
commercial
and moral.**

we leave moral and religious questions to the proper authorities, and confine our attention to the realism of buying and selling. The word "business" is used in a wide sense, so as to include every occupation, whether professional or commercial. However much a professional man may flatter himself that he is not "in trade," he cannot deny the emphatic need there is for handling his professional duties in a business-like manner. To this extent, therefore, he and the commercial man pure and simple are on the same footing, and the rules of action are applicable to both.

**Our point of view.** Stated in other words, our point of view is a study of those ways and means by which we can achieve the best possible results in our daily calling. Naturally, each calling has its peculiarly distinguishing features, and an excellency in one may be a weakness in another; but apart from these differences, there are underlying principles which are common to all working activities, and we shall endeavour to expound them. The art of success, as here conceived, has two constituent properties, *knowledge* and *action;* the knowledge to consist of an intimate ac-

quaintance with the present condition and
future possibilities of some department of
money-making activity, and the action to lie
in executive capacity for carrying schemes to
a favourable conclusion.

# CHAPTER III

## IS SUCCESS INCREASINGLY DIFFICULT?

*"The more powerful the obstacle, the more glory we have in overcoming it."*—MOLIÈRE.

QUITE recently we put this question to a bluff, hearty, and, in some senses, very successful man, and he replied: "Nonsense! The idea is preposterous. Success is as easy of attain-

**Yes and No.** ment now as it ever was. What difference can time make?" We also put the question to another man, a hard-headed Scot, fresh from a big commercial battle in which he had been victorious. Said he: "I am inclined to answer 'Yes.' Success comes more readily to some workers than it does to others, and they are inclined to take their own experience as a universal guide. This is false reasoning."

Now, which of these two men is right? They are both stalwarts, but they do not agree on a matter of opinion; and yet the truth must be in one of them, or else it lies between

16

them.  For ourselves, we think the truth lies
between them, partly because the question has
nothing to say as to the kind of individual for
whom success is increasingly difficult, and
partly because no satisfactory answer can be
given in the direct negative or affirmative.
Still, it is only by discussing the matter generally that these points can be cleared up, and
naturally enough the first item that claims attention is the alarming growth of competition.
It grows because it is inevitable.  We may
read of Ideal Republics where kings  **The growth of**
are philosophers, of Utopias where  **competition.**
harmonies soothe competing elements to rest,
and of Vision Cities where supply and demand
are worked by State machinery; but they
never convince us—they are not sufficiently
attractive.   Not that competition itself is
attractive — far from it.   Sometimes it is
nothing short of being horrible, so ghastly
are the details in some branches of what has
been aptly called " trade murder."   But, after
all, it is the abuse of the competitive method
which produces lamentable results; and if on
the one hand we are to escape reducing life
to a sort of mechanism, and on the other hand

to desist from a price-cutting which can only end in disaster, we must resolve to use the competitive method, and neither abolish it nor abuse it.

The fact is, competition has come to stay. The trust system may reduce its intensity in **Trusts and** certain quarters for a time, but no or-
**combines.** ganisation, however cunningly devised and financially supported, can uproot the tendency in man to compete with his fellows. Competition is Darwinism, the law of the survival of the fittest. It is the major fact in the story of the world of Nature, and since man is part of Nature's scheme, he finds that the struggle for existence is not a fossil discovery of some past era, but a living reality of the twentieth century. So far from appearing to decrease in vital force, competition shows very evident signs of increase. The population is an important factor to be considered, especially in its relation to the size of the country. With the exception of Belgium, there are more people to the square mile in England than anywhere else in the world. This seething mass of humanity must live somehow; and even though the multiplication of people means the

multiplication of wants, it is equally true that more people means more competition.

Some time ago there appeared in a London morning paper an advertisement for a secretary. Five hundred men applied for the vacant post. Just think of it! Each applicant **Five hundred for one vacancy.** had one chance among five hundred— that is, if we consider the matter from the standpoint of numbers. In the same way if only twenty had applied the chances of success would have been greatly augmented. But mere numbers do not decide the real intensity of competition; they rather show the state of the market in any particular kind of demand and supply. The real intensity is decided by the number of competent candidates. Let us take a case in point.

A merchant requiring a clerk recently inserted the following advertisement in a leading newspaper :—

CLERK, smart, wanted. Good chance for a man who understands his work thoroughly. Shorthand a recommendation. State salary expected, qualifications, &c., to ——.

The advertisement was published every day for a week in the same journal, and the number of replies received was 103. An analysis of the applications for the position revealed many interesting things. Out of the **A mass of incompetency.** 103, ten were absolutely undecipherable, and the writers of these would without doubt call themselves clerks. Another half-dozen of the replies were so smeared with blots and alterations that they might also be included with the ten just mentioned. Out of the whole lot there were not more than a score of good penmen. Over half of the applications were faulty, either in spelling or grammar, or perhaps in both. Two or three of the applicants were under the impression that there was only one " p " in apply, while another one or two spelt it " applie." There were two candidates who when writing in the first person used the small letter " i." The following orthographical errors were also noticed : " servises," " bookeeping," " comand," " hopeing," " knowlege," " here " (for hear), " there " (for their), and " shortand." One individual proudly boasted of the fact that he had a slight knowledge of " Frensh." Apparently he had also a slight knowledge of English, although he did not mention the fact.[1]

[1] *How and Where to Find a Situation*, by G. E. Skerry.

Now the five hundred applicants for the secretaryship before mentioned would undoubtedly be able to exhibit a higher standard of English composition than the " clerks," but the likelihood is that fully one half of them had no right to apply at all.  It is simply astounding to observe on what slender grounds of ability and experience many men think themselves competent to hold important offices with their accruing salaries.  Probably a desirable salary is the cause of a large percentage of applications from incompetents; but, whether this be so or not, the number of men **Mere numbers** who present themselves as candidates **no criterion.** for a vacancy is no criterion of the intensity of competition.  The proper question is: Does competency in all classes of occupation grow so quickly that good men are often without a berth?  The man who is poorly equipped and the mediocre man—neither bad nor good —will often be without employment; but is this the case with a really capable man?  No; he will nearly always be in work; but capability is an increasing characteristic of labour, both clerical and mechanical, and one result of this is that he cannot so easily obtain the

scope he requires; for the number of places
to be filled does not multiply so rapidly as the

**Vacancies for the competent.** number of men who can fill them. It
is just here that the keenness of com-
petition among subordinate workers is
felt the most. Ability, energy, and character
will nearly always bring a man to the top, but
one can admit this and yet believe that the path
becomes more difficult every year. The cry
to-day is Educate, Educate, Educate, and although it used to be a species of objectionable
cant, it is now a serious gospel with many
earnest prophets engaged in its proclamation.
Technical classes of every kind are held in
most of our towns and cities; slowly but surely
the country is awakening to a sense of the
importance of advanced commercial instruc-
tion; and the effect of the improvements made
in the past, and now manifest in the present,
goes to show that competency, already pro-
gressing, will in the future tend to become
more and more the normal condition of English labour.

But some one says: " Granting that the real
intensity of competition lies in the struggle
between an increasing number of competent

men, is it true that the places to be filled do not increase in a corresponding ratio?" It *is* true; and here is the proof. The tendency of business in this country and America, more particularly the latter, is to consolidate itself into large houses. The small man, employing a moderate number of clerks and operatives, cannot compete successfully with a large trust working on colossal, and therefore more economical, lines. The movement in all classes of trade is towards the "combine," and this results in the wiping-out of lesser enterprises and the multiplication of responsible posts in big enterprises carrying very high salaries. There never was a time when a man in the position of a manager could earn as much as he can to-day. Thus the president of a large American Trust said not long ago: "I am anxious at the present time to fill five positions, three of which would yield £3000 a year and the other two £2000 each. If the right men could be found they could step into these places and these salaries to-morrow." [1]  Another Trust

*Business consolidation.*

*American testimony.*

[1] *Are Young Men's Chances Less?* (*The World's Work*, p. 171, Dec., 1900).

President says: "Highly developed organisations, resulting in an enormous volume of business, have increased the necessity for intelligence; and, since the supply of brains is not equal to the demand, the price of brains has risen." Exactly. There are finer openings now than ever before for men who can manage departments in great businesses, but, naturally, those openings are not exceedingly plentiful, and what there are of them seem difficult to fill. Such a condition of things is good news to the capable and ambitious; but this tendency to pay large salaries to a few men, and very moderate ones to the rest, can hardly be said to increase the average chances of success. It means a fierce struggle for the higher appointments, whether the struggle be justified by merit on the part of the competitors or not; and as the higher appointments are necessarily a limited quantity, the competent worker cannot always receive the full reward of his powers—in fact, it is abundantly evident that the achievement of success demands a combination of gifts more rare than hitherto, coupled with an adroit energy, to which the past generation of people were almost strangers.

**Larger salaries to fewer men.**

And if this be true of men in salaried positions, it is equally true of men in business.
The tendency, previously referred to, of
trade to become centred in large houses **The small
man in
business.**
affects the smaller man in two ways.
First, if he is already in business he finds it
impossible to compete with the large houses,
and, second, if he wishes to launch out for
himself he finds that more capital is needed
than was once the case; hence success is an
increasingly difficult problem. A man can
still make a living in a small way of trade, and
even find time to attend football matches; if
he sticks close to business early and late he
may achieve a moderate success; but if he
would enlarge his concerns on an impressive
scale he must make business his religion for
seven days a week. The greatest chances for
the smaller man, as opposed to the large houses,
are not in the cities, but in the smaller towns;
and here, of course, the possibilities are decided
by the size of the population; for if a certain
line of enterprise, in one particular place,
affords a living for a hundred people, and
five hundred make an attempt to live and
prosper, it is manifest that the struggle will

become as keen as in the heart of a great city.

Years ago, in some businesses, £10,000 was **Need of** a good sum with which to commence **capital.** operations; nowadays, five times that amount is considered barely sufficient. This is a serious handicap; for if a man has a peculiar genius for some branch of trade, a genius which can only show itself when he has an absolutely free hand, and not as the servant of a Trust, it means that lack of capital decides his destiny unless he rouses himself to superhuman effort. Of course, such effort indicates the increasing difficulty of success. The large houses threaten the smaller houses already in existence, and strangle those that have just been born. This change in the basis of commercialism is nowhere more evident than in the use of the word *independence*. At one time it loomed large in our vocabulary, and connoted wonderful things to our imagination. Private owners of great industries were said to be "independent"; they could do as they liked with their own. It is not the same now. The volume of business becomes too great for the single individual, and a company is formed to divide the responsibility. Independence then vanishes, and it looks as if the day of the one-man concern has gone by for ever. One-man genius may develop the work up to a certain stage, but so soon as that has been reached other intelligences step in to assist in the expansion of what is already too unwieldy for a single brain. "Complete independence," says the man of the Trust, "is only found in the wigwam of the Indian. Was Captain Clark less the commander, or Chief Engineer Milligan less the engineer, because they were dependent upon each other in making the historic run and the fine fight of the *Oregon* in the Spanish-American War? Each gave the other his opportunity. While economic evolution is centralising production in large corporations, decentralisation of ownership goes on simultaneously through the rapid distribution of shares."

**The vogue of the company.**

**Division of responsibility.**

Yes; independence is going, and this is how another American writer defends the new *régime:* "There are three sorts of men, and for two of these sorts the tendency to industrial consolidation is a distinct advantage, while

for the third there is no salvation in any
economic system that has yet been devised.

The plea of<br>the Trusts. These three classes are: the thoroughly
competent, who go to the top, and
command salaries that would once have been
fortunes; the half-competent, who find profitable employment in subordinate positions,
and are saved from going into business for
themselves and failing, as they would have
fallen under the old system; and the incompetent, who sit on the park benches, as they
would have done before." [1]    There is something very *naïve* about this classification of
men.    Is competency only found in great
organisations, and do none but the half-competent begin for themselves?    How delicious
is that sentiment which defends the Trust by
showing how it saves men from setting up on
their own account—*and failing!*  No; competition is making things harder all round, for
although it offers a greater number of posts
with dazzling salaries, it decreases the number
of places with moderately high salaries; and
the advent of the big combine presses heavily
on the small man, whilst it tends to crush

[1] *Are Young Men's Chances Less?* p. 172.

independent enterprise altogether.   The process of trade consolidation may be inevitable,
and, in the general sense, it may be beneficial
to the public as a purchaser, but for the great
multitude who aim at material prosperity it
seems to lessen chances which in the past
generations were more numerous.

Success in life is increasingly difficult for
other reasons than the growth of competition.
"Some things have been done so well
they can hardly be done better."  However one may object to the conservatism
of this sentence, it would be foolish to deny
that it contains much truth.   Take the field of
literature.  Dr. C. H. Pearson in his *National
Life and Character* says it is absolutely certain
that in poetry certain subjects are never to
be taken again, and instances the tale of
Troy, the *Inferno, Faust,* and *Paradise Lost.*
Whether this be true or not, it is more than
highly probable that the achievements of
Homer, Dante, Goethe, and Milton have made
greater success a matter of superlative difficulty.  He who would succeed as a poet or
prose-writer — in the artistic sense — has a
well-nigh superhuman task before him, not

*Success and past achievements.*

only because there are so many respectable versifiers and essayists, but because in some departments the limits of excellence have already been reached, at any rate so far as we can judge. *Will* there be another essay as good as *Dream Children?* There *may* be, but we shall have to wait for another Charles Lamb.

**Newspapers.** Take daily newspapers as another illustration. So long as all daily journals charged one penny for a copy, there was room for a paper at a halfpenny; and once the halfpenny paper had obtained a firm footing by reason of its ingenuity and enterprise, people began to think of farthing newspapers. But the halfpenny paper is now done so well, it would be difficult to improve on it at a cheaper rate, even supposing farthings were more popular in the general currency than they are. These facts go to show that daily journalism has almost reached its final stage as to cheapness and the efficiency of news distribution; and the man who would essay to succeed in the production of a better and cheaper article has difficulties to face which the halfpenny promoters never dreamt of. In weekly journalism we still wait for the penny *Spectator*.

But it is mainly in the arts of literature that " some things have been done so well they can hardly be done better." In business **No finality** there is no finality, judging by the **in business.** wonders in the way of improvements that are made yearly. The mental outlook of the most progressive Americans is one which prohibits the idea of present perfection. They always believe in the possibility of a better way, and for this reason work their machinery with ruthless disregard of preserving its endurance, simply because they expect it will soon be thrown on the scrap heap on account of some better invention. Such an outlook is the proper one to cultivate, but as efficiency increases, greater demands are made on the man who would go one better. The production of artificial light, from the torch **The difficulty** to the electric globe, is an interesting **of advance.** story, but the production of better and cheaper light than the Edison-Swan-Incandescent calls for learning and experience in an altogether new and advanced degree. When the steam-engine arrived, people said that the problem of locomotion had been finally solved, but others kept an open mind; and it may be that soon electric traction will everywhere be a serious competitor. Still, the difficulties in the way are great, and, so soon as they are overcome, greater difficulties will have to be reckoned with on the part of those who attempt further improvements.

.   .   .   .   .

We have tried to show that success in the sense we have defined is increasingly difficult. Competition is keener because of the growing number of competent men, and the struggle is accentuated by the tendency towards the consolidating of business in Trusts and Combines; so that, whilst a few men can earn appetising salaries, the rest are compelled to fight harder for the figure they would have reached if the huge business did not either outbid their prices, or put the veto on starting an independent though smaller enterprise. Again, every fresh advance towards economical efficiency calls for a higher standard of educated experience on the part of those who aim at still higher efficiency.

*Summary of results.*

But there is another side to the picture. Difficulty does not argue impossibility. The
light-hearted, airy way in which some **Difficulty not impossibility.**
successful men have explained their achieve-
ments, and told others the trick is easy when
once you know it, requires an emphatic negative, as well as an exposition of the real truth,
such as we have attempted to give. Nevertheless, there is no reason for any one except the
severely handicapped, to be pessimistic. The
more difficult the task, the greater the rewards
of victory. Success has never been easy at any
time, and if it is harder now than before, that
fact can only double the interest and excite-
ment of the struggle. The spirit to cultivate
is that of Napoleon when he was told the Alps
were in the way of his army's progress. Said
he: " Then there shall be no Alps."

# CHAPTER IV

## LUCK? OR NO LUCK?

*" Good luck is another name for tenacity of purpose."*—EMERSON.

"LUCK" is one of the most abused words in the English language. Everybody uses it, more or less, and very few people are free from using it in an altogether incorrect manner. The man who starts a new branch **The word** establishment, which, after a time, comes **as used.** to grief, says he has been unlucky; the man who speculates on the Stock Exchange in shares which he knows to be full of risk, and loses heavily, says his luck has deserted him; the general who chases a flying enemy and encumbers his movements with pianos and kitchen ranges, the result being that his rearguard is unexpectedly cut up, complains of his " rank bad luck." Every man who gets on is lucky; every man who does not is held back by the iron hand of Fate.

34

What is the truth about this matter? Does success depend on luck entirely? or partly? or not at all? To answer these questions we must first understand the meaning of the word itself. Usually, it means anything that happens either to our advantage or disadvantage—*good* luck; *bad* luck. If we catch a train because it happens to be late, or chance to be carrying an umbrella when it rains, or take our holidays during fine weather, we are said to be *lucky*. Conversely, anything that happens to our disadvantage renders us *un*-lucky. In this colloquial use of the word there are traces of the real truth. Luck is essentially a result arising out of the play of powers over which we have no control. A farmer does not count himself lucky if, on sowing wheat, he reaps wheat; it **Luck and Nature.** is a fixed law, allowing no chances whatever, that as is the sowing, so also the reaping. But if the farmer sows wheat and the elements are against him, inasmuch as his fields are either flooded with the rains or scorched up by the fierce sun, he may well call himself unlucky. He sowed the seed and must take his chances at the hands of Nature.

Here, then, is one instance where success and failure depend largely on what we may call extra-human agencies. The agriculturist may use the best seed it is possible to buy, he may employ the most skilled labour his means can afford, the very latest implements may be requisitioned for his service, but, after working early and late, he is bound to admit that the final issue—good or bad—is at the mercy of the heavens.

It is much the same with the voyage of a trading vessel across the ocean. The builder of the vessel may have used the best materials in the most approved manner, the captain and the crew may be as skilful as it is possible for mariners to be, the cargo may be so well stored as to be beyond the risk of "shifting," but for all that a successful termination of the voyage depends greatly on favourable wind and weather. In the days of sailing vessels navigation was almost wholly at the mercy of Nature's forces, and luck was consequently a larger factor than it is to-day, when steam power has brought dangerous elements within a narrower area of control. How far is this true of other men in other

*Luck and a voyage.*

occupations? Is the mechanic, or the merchant, or the lawyer dependent upon outside
influences like the farmer, or the captain of a
sailing vessel? Certainly not; for the farther
we are from Nature the less scope there is for
the play of chance, simply because civilisation
is a human creation and its laws are consequently more easily within our own control.
For instance, the colliery proprietor is one
degree less at the mercy of Nature than the
farmer; for, whereas the latter must put up
with the ever-changing caprice of sun and rain,
the former has only to contend with the past
caprice of a geological era. Still, the opening
of a new mine is necessarily attended with many
chances of good or bad luck. The samples of
coal obtained may be of the best and the **Luck and**
supply apparently unlimited; the newest **geology.**
machinery may be set up and the miners paid
at a high rate of wages; and sales may be
both rapid and profitable. But what if at the
end of three months a " fault " is discovered?
It probably means that the missing seam will
have to be re-discovered at a great expense of
time and money; indeed, it may mean that the
proprietor must sell his property or seek the

D

aid of a capitalist.  Mining, therefore, depends
for its failure or success on facts beyond our
ken, at any rate so far as hidden mineral
wealth is concerned; but so soon as the proprietor enters the coal market he lessens his
risks until they are at a minimum.  He will
engage to supply coal continuously at the rate
of tons a day, even though there is a possibility of the miners coming out on strike in a
few months' time.  A strike is one of those
contingencies which can be provided for, and
the contract is made on the express condition
that the proprietor is not responsible for delivery so long as the men refuse to work.
This will serve as an illustration of the theory
previously stated: that the farther we get
from Nature the less room there is for the
play of luck.  The colliery owner must submit to his luck in burrowing underground,
but in selling his coal to others he need not
submit to the penalties of a contract which
obliges him to supply fuel during the time of
an unlucky strike.  Nature's contingencies can
only be accepted as they occur; commercial
contingencies are easily met by specific stipu-
lation or by some form of insurance.

At this point we shall have to meet an objection.  It will be urged that, if luck is less operative the farther we get from Nature, what is to be said of luck in buying and selling shares on the Stock Exchange? **Luck on the Stock Exchange.** Is it not evident that there, in the very heart of finance and civilisation, luck is almost the supreme thing?  No; certainly not.  In operations on the Stock Exchange there are many *chances* of fortune and misfortune, but there is, properly speaking, no luck at all.  Luck is the happy, or unhappy, play of powers over which we have no control, and which will act upon us whether we will or not, and irrespective of our merit or demerit.  Now a man need have nothing to do with stocks and shares, and consequently the rise and fall of prices will not disturb him in the least.  On the other hand, the farmer is bound to accept the luck of propitious or unpropitious weather; he would rather that the excellence of crops did not depend on outside agencies so much as they do, but he cannot help himself; unwillingly he is compelled to take his chance.  That is where he is separated from the Stock Exchange speculator, for the latter takes his chance willingly; he deliberately imports risk into his business and is prepared to abide by the consequences. Of course in some cases he can foresee these consequences and manipulate his stock accordingly, but whatever be the result, fortunate or unfortunate, the method is closely akin to all deliberate games of chance: *it is a gamble.*

There is a second objection to be met. Some one argues that luck is quite as much

Luck and<br>civilisation. a fact of civilisation as of Nature, and adduces the following as an illustration. A discouraged young man was returning home from a most unprofitable day in the city, and when about to step into a 'bus at Charing Cross noticed an elderly woman trip and fall almost under the horses' feet. He at once ran to her assistance, and finding she was somewhat seriously hurt, called a cab and took her to the hospital. He left his name and address with the porter and proceeded home, feeling perhaps a little more disconsolate on account of his association with this accident. Next day his business affairs took a better turn; then they became bad again, until at the end of three months bankruptcy stared him in the face. But one morning the postman brought him—well, everybody knows the story—the elderly lady had died and left him a large fortune. And we are asked, " Is not this a specimen of genuine luck?" Most certainly it is if we take the usual interpretation of the word—not otherwise. Luck presupposes an absence of merit or demerit in the recipient, and if the elderly lady had resolved to leave her fortune to the first man whose name she saw on opening a London Directory, that man would be a genuinely lucky man. But our distressed young man of business did something for the money he received. True, the service was not equal to the number of pounds sterling which swelled his all but extinct balance at the bankers'; and in this disparity between the service and the reward lies the real element of luck. But it must not be forgotten that the sudden accession of wealth had its starting-point in an act of human sympathy, the execution of which many men would have left to the policeman. Of course humane actions which end in nothing more than a letter of thanks, or a box of cigars, or even no thanks and no cigars, cannot

be regarded as *un*lucky; the laws of brotherhood do not decree a return in cash value.

In purely commercial affairs luck is often
accorded an exaggerated position. We do

not deny that, seemingly, opportunities
**Luck in**
**oppor-**      to succeed have a peculiar tendency to
**tunities.**
knock at the door of one man in particular, as if there were some subtle relation
between them and the man whose admittance
they seek. One might be inclined to think that
here was the whole truth: opportunities are
drawn by the magnetism of a strong personality
—in other words, chances congregate where
there is the greatest capacity. But if so, where
does the element of luck come in? So far
from being luck, it would appear to be law.
Besides, is it not a fact that glorious opportunities crowd at the doors of the lazy and
incompetent, and the lazy and incompetent
send them empty away?

The real question is, "How far does commercial success depend on agencies over which
we have no control?" The answer is,
**Success does**
**not depend**    "Very little." We do not minimise
**on luck.**
difficulties, and the right-about-face
movements which a new invention may cause

in some industries, but, speaking generally, the forces which regulate business progress are well within the control of an alert mind. Even when it is admitted that some occupations are more remunerative than others, that in the same branch of trade equally well conceived schemes result in great divergencies of profit, that fraud and cunning seem more than a match for honest dealing, and that to many men openings "come" which others seek in vain—the broad truth still remains: success is achieved by men of superior mind and character, more often the latter than the former. Luck in business is an affair of "seeming" and "appearing"; but the deeper one probes the matter, the less dominant is luck and the more dominant is law.

The genuinely unlucky man is not so plentiful as is sometimes imagined, but he can be met with occasionally. Here is one, who **The real** was apprehended by the police owing to **unlucky man.** his likeness to a certain individual "wanted" for several reasons. The mistake was afterwards evident, but the unfortunate man had suffered much on account of his undeserved humiliation—in fact, the mental shock of being

led by constables through crowded streets
almost deprived him of his reason; actually,
it handicapped him in the race of life, and put
the veto on a most promising career. Things
happen just as happily to other men. They
have, to begin with, the best of heredities and
environments; friends appear at opportune
moments and render them invaluable service;
nobody wrongly introduces the scapegoat element into their lives; and nothing seems to
be wanting to make life happy and successful. Why is this? Is there any law behind
the process? Well, there is no law beyond

**The mystery of luck.** Nature's to decide whether a man shall
be born of physically diseased and
financially poor parents, or the reverse; but
Maeterlinck suggests that there is a law after
all, although we cannot trace its *raison d'être*.
He does not attempt to explain the mystery;
he contents himself with the statement that
we carry about with us an unconscious life
which—unwittingly to us—predisposes some
to disaster and others to success. Consequently between the man and the region of
fact wherein lie the germs of success there
is a subtle sympathy, and in the same way

between the man and the region of fact wherein lie the germs of failure there is a like subtle sympathy.

Maeterlinck's theory is nothing more than reincarnation, or, to be accurate, the Law of Karma, which says that our past earth lives are continually affecting us for evil or for good. Karma is a clever guess at one of the riddles of existence, but it still remains to be proved to the Western mind. So the riddle must remain a riddle; moreover, it is scarcely within our province, here and now, to say what place human inequalities may have in a system of Divine government; our purview is confined to events as they affect earthly prosperity, and not with their final solution.

Returning to the questions with which the discussion commenced, it is clear that **A theory of** there are some occupations in which **luck stated.** luck plays a definite part; whilst all occupations are not without elements of chance, but for which it is possible to make some sort of provision. And since the majority of callings are connected with the facts of civilisation, as distinct from the facts of Nature, it follows,

as a matter of course, that only a very few
people can blame their bad luck for their want
of success. Look on the other side of the
medal. Does it not say that much of our
so-called luck is really a clever but human
anticipation of events that were likely to
happen at a particular time? Take the
following as an illustration. A pro-
vincial town had grown so rapidly that
the streets leading to the market-place became
insufficient for the needs of the traffic, and the
Corporation determined to cut a new street of
considerable width on the south side of the
market square. When the plans came out it
was seen that all the house property to be
demolished belonged to one man, who was
little beloved by the Council or by anybody
else. He was called " an awfully lucky fellow,"
as the compensation allowed was a great deal
in excess of the value of the property. But
*was* he lucky? Not he. " I foresaw," he
said, " that a new outlet for traffic would soon
be absolutely necessary, and I also foresaw
that the only possible outlet would be on the
south side; therefore I quietly purchased all
the houses I wanted and waited my time."

**Luck and prophetic insight.**

Exactly. Whatever protest may be made against money-getting of this type, it affords an insight into the working of much that passes as "luck." The principals of the great newspaper and periodical syndicates of to-day are often described as "lucky." True, their enterprises have succeeded, but only because they were clearly and cleverly conceived, and carried out with intelligent energy. There is nothing more irritating than the simple way in which the average man reduces a remarkable achievement to its lowest common denominator. This is how he does it. "One day a commercial traveller in the north of England thought he would start a weekly paper on certain lines. After making suitable preparations, he published the first issue in due course, and the public was delighted with it. The idea was quite a lucky hit. Of course the traveller left his round at once, and has been raking in the shekels ever since."

**Successful men always "lucky."**

With what smug complacency does this critic explain his own lack of success when he enlarges on that of others! He cannot—or will not—see that a weekly paper on " certain

lines," and one with which the public is
"delighted," could only arise out of much
previous observation and reflection; and that
"suitable preparations" demand considerable
powers of organisation. No; it was sheer
luck; otherwise the critic would have been at
the top of the tree himself—long ago.

Women are said to be more superstitious
than men, but professional palmists and fortune-
tellers number a great many among their clients
who would resent classification as a "weaker
vessel." Deep down in the heart they have an
unspoken conviction that success is a whim
**Luck and** of destiny; we are either under the in-
**superstition.** fluence of a beneficent planetary god or
the stars in their courses fight against us. No
words are too strong to condemn a mental outlook so pessimistic. That there are mysteries
in life goes without saying, but it is impossible
to plead destiny as an excuse for failure until
the last effort has been put forth. As to why
opportunities sometimes crowd themselves into
one man's life, and not another's, we may not
be able to say, but for all that we can have
little patience with the six-foot giant, sound
in wind and limb, and possessed of average

abilities, who whimpers: "I'm unlucky. You can't fight destiny."

You can't? What did Wendell Phillips say? "Common sense bows to the inevitable *and makes use of it.*" Note those words in italics. The reader has had to submit to the inevitable before now, but did he ever make use of it? The Scotch piper at the battle of Dargai was brought to the ground by a shot from the enemy's lines. He might well have ceased to fight, but, submitting to the inevitable, he made use of it by playing a tune to cheer his comrades, despite the rain of bullets around him. Destiny threw him down, but soul was master all the time. In his *Tess of the D'Urbervilles* Thomas Hardy closes a brilliant narrative with these words: "And the President of the Immortals had finished his sport with Tess." Without descending to unworthy criticism of a great master, we may be permitted to say that sentiment of this kind is only too readily accepted by the weak as an apology for their lack of achievement; they are, they say, the sport of the gods. On others the effect is quite the reverse. They develop a kind of pride in

*How to meet disasters.*

resisting the hand of Fate; they resolve that
the President of the Immortals shall accomplish
his designs with the utmost possible difficulty;
and that, if there is to be any sport, man shall
have his share of it. There is nothing ir-
reverent in such an attitude. If the facts of
life are irrational, and based on the pranks of
a sporting God whose legitimate fun is human
agony and women's tears, then let every man
resist to the uttermost, and say—

I am master of my Fate
And I am captain of my Soul.

**Fatalism.** The literature of fatalism is plentiful, and
in some respects convincing, but its
writers forget that we learn as much from our
illusions as from our knowledge. We need
no sermons on the littleness and impotence
of man, as contrasted with the greatness and
power of the universe; but we do need homi-
lies that shall urge men not to be what
Carlyle describes as "forked radishes," or, in
other words, puppets, the strings of whose
movements are in the hands of Fate.

No; this whimpering about "Just my luck"
will never do. It is one thing to be foolish

and beat your head against a wall; it is quite
another to sit down and mope over an unex-
pected turn in the game of life.   Even if life
is regarded as an enemy, it is all the more
reason why you should re-enter the fray and
win, or even if you fail in the attempt, it is
better to fail in action than to succeed in lazy
acquiescence.

It is not in our stars,
But in ourselves that we are underlings.

# CHAPTER V

## THE HANDICAP OF LIMITATIONS

*" Commerce is a game of skill which
every man cannot play."*—EMERSON.

THAT somewhat wearisome phrase, " Heredity and Environment," is full of meaning when considered in reference to the problems of success. So much depends on inherited physical, mental, and moral qualities, and so much on the surroundings of the place in which our lot is cast, that the hackneyed phrase just quoted is replete with suggestions for every aspiring youth.

But one would think, from the way in which books have been written and speeches made, that there are no limitations in the race for success, and that *every* man may win either wealth or fame if he be so disposed. The only limitation, it would seem, is indolence.

Such talk can only be described as mischievous. It is mischievous because Rose-water optimism. it places a false ideal, or rather an impossible one, before the minds of those who have less than ordinary ability: and because it reduces the quality of great achievements until they become possible to the incompetent. No optimism which denies facts as we find them is worthy of a moment's attention.

"Get up early, retire early, and stick to business: that is my recipe for success," Recipes for success. says a millionaire. An ambitious youth, struck with its simplicity, tries the recipe with unfailing courage for a year or two, and at the end of that period is able to report improvement, but success is still a long way off. He has done all that the millionaire asked him to do; he retired early and rose early, and never grudged his employer an extra hour at the office. Nevertheless, when a new assistant-secretary was wanted, the employer brought in a man from the outside, and the ambitious youth's chance was gone—for that time at least. He is much discouraged, and begins to think that "men who have risen" either do not know the secret of their success, or else they pur-

E

posely conceal it—a thought that possibly has more truth in it than is generally supposed.

We have all read symposia by prosperous merchants, telling us the secret of prosperity.

**More "secrets."** It lies in " patience," or " perseverance," or " caution," or " hard work," or all these plus something else, and we have only to do as the writers have done and we shall receive a like reward. The great defect of this kind of optimism is that it is so utterly indiscriminate, and ignores altogether the personal equation. It raises false hopes by suggesting that success is one of the simples of existence, and its possession within the reach of every one. The emphasis on moral virtues is right in its place, but we shall see later that unless a man can strike out in a new direction all the work in the world will

**The real facts obscured.** do little to further him; he might as well try to bale out the Atlantic. Anybody who takes the trouble to analyse these short and easy methods advocated by millionaires and others will see how inadequate they are for the purpose intended. True, they inspire hope, and that is better than creating despair; but is it not much better

still to state the real facts and leave every
man to judge and act for himself? As a rule,
and for some occult reason, the marvellously
successful man does not know how he came
to be great in worldly possessions, and when
called upon to write on the subject he generally indulges in the Higher Optimism and
gives his readers the impression that fortune
will soon be in their grasp. Modesty is
perhaps at the bottom of this kind of talk,
but it is far wiser to adopt the policy of Mr.
Andrew Carnegie, who seems to know **Andrew**
only too well where he has scored **Carnegie.**
above his fellows. When asked his price for
a magazine article on " How to Organise," he
replied, " £1,000,000." And he meant it! not
as a specific contract with an editor, for what
editor could write a cheque for a million? but
as an indication of the cost of learning his
particular secret of success. Compare Mr.
Carnegie with the Higher Optimists. Would
you not rather know the solid truth than start
off with theories that may prove delusive?

No; there is no " success tabloid " **No " success**
that will suit everybody. You may **tabloid."**
listen to speeches that inspire the heart, and

read books that arouse enthusiasm, but at the
last you will find you have to draw your own
map, formulate your own ideas, and determine

**Form your own plan.** your own plan of action. It is better
so. You do not want to live on another
man's recipe, nor do you need to despise it.
Make your own, for it will take into account
your abilities—a fact which the Higher Optimism complacently ignores. Desire is not the
measure of capability, and when misleading
utterances cause desire to rise too high, the sub-
sequent fall is perilous in the extreme. But let
us deal with the subject of limitations more
directly.

Physical limitations naturally come first.
Few men have been able to overcome the handicap of a frail or diseased body. Cardinal Riche-
lieu is a brilliant exception, but the list is inca-
pable of much extension; whereas, on the other
hand, there is a magnificent list of great men who
were physically stalwart, and the presumption is
that minus this blessing they would not have

**The drain on physical energy.** achieved what they did. Think for a
moment of the intensity of business life
to-day. The strain upon nerve and brain
is tremendous. Only strong men can hope to

keep up with the competition that grows apace.
It has been cynically observed that to succeed at
the Bar the first requisite is to be a good animal,
the second is to have a slight knowledge of
the law and a deep knowledge of human
nature, and the third is to marry a solicitor's
daughter.  The first requisite is one which
holds good everywhere, and however well-edu-
cated a man may be, however noble in character and disposition, if he be a poor animal
he must recognise the fact and act accordingly.
There is little room to-day for the individual
who is "always ailing," or the man who,
though passably strong, is continually alco-
holised on account of an inherited weakness
in that direction.  Such men are to be pitied,
but there can be no question about the effect
of these limitations on their chances of success.  Hazlitt in the *Plain Speaker*
enumerates constitutional talent as one **Hazlitt on constitutional talent.**
of the requisites of a progressive career.
"By constitutional talent I mean in general
the warmth and vigour given to a man's ideas
and pursuits by his bodily stamina.  A weak
mind in a sound body is better, or at least
more profitable, than a sound mind in a weak

and crazy conformation.  How many instances
might I quote!  Let a man have a quick circu-
lation, a good digestion, the bulk, and thews,
and sinews of a man, and the alacrity, the
unthinking confidence inspired by these; and
without an atom, a shadow of the *mens
divinior* he shall strut and swagger and
vapour and jostle his way through life, and
have the upper hand of those who are his
betters in everything but health and strength.
His jests shall be echoed with loud laughter
because his own lungs begin to crow, like
chanticleer, before he has uttered them; while
a little, hectic, nervous humorist shall stammer
out an admirable conceit that is damned in
the  doubtful  delivery."    Hazlitt  naturally
draws his type from the world of letters, but
it is a type which well illustrates the entire
species.  Do we not all know the timid individual, excellent in character, and ready to do
any one a good turn, and yet never a prosperous man himself?  Why is it?  Because, to
put the matter in everyday phrase, however
good an engine is, it is no good if you have no
steam to drive it.  A retiring, diffident disposition is not necessarily the outcome of bodily

weakness, but, as temperament is destiny, such a disposition consigns its possessor to a sphere where action means less than thought, and sufficiency more than riches.

Can nothing then be done? Are we to submit meekly to the kind of body given to us, and acquiesce in all its disadvantages? There can be no doubt about the sub-  **What to do.** mission. We are bound to accept what is given to us, but there is no need in the world why we should acquiesce in disadvantages. Johnson did not allow his hypochondria to conquer him; Pascal patiently endured the fiery vision that haunted him in consequence of an overtaxed mind; Milton sang in spite of his blindness; and many a lesser star, handicapped, not midway, but from the very start, has done much to overcome the veto which physical disabilities had placed upon progress. Bow to the inevitable, but make use of it.

Mental capacity may, for our purposes, be divided into genius, talent, and average ability; and the simple rule in business is that, other things being equal, the best brains score the greatest triumph. The majority of us have neither genius nor talent: we belong to the thousands that possess average ability; why, then, should we be surprised if our cleverer comrades with a sounder judgment, a keener insight, a more masterly grasp of detail, and immeasurably superior advantages of education, forge on ahead, whilst we trudge on slowly behind? Would it not surprise us more if we left *them* behind? and yet these optimistic men of money calmly state that any man can succeed in acquiring wealth if he will only be "truthful," or "an early riser," or something of that kind. Such expressions may be allowed to pass as pleasantries in an attempt to evade an exposition of the secret of success, but as sincere contributions to the truth they are as harmful as they are false. Theoretically, the position we have stated is unassailable; the best brains win, other things being equal. It often happens, however, that the "other things" are not equal. When we analyse the successful man, we frequently find he has not marked mental ability, except in one well-defined direction; in other respects he is perhaps less than ordinary. As for the failures—they are not unusually men of brilliant gifts. How is

*Genius, talent and average ability.*

*The best brains win.*

this? It is only another aspect of the handicap of limitations. The man of moderate
brain-power has probably a talent for industry
and possesses great strength of will. The
man with commercial instincts of a high order
is occasionally a whimsical being, splendid in
ideas, but lax and inconstant in execution.
No man, therefore, need plead average ability
as an explanation of his failure.

"One of the most important lessons that
experience teaches is that, on the whole,
and in the great majority of cases, **Character
greater than
ability.**
success in life depends more on character than on either intellect or fortune. Many
brilliant exceptions, no doubt, tend to obscure
the rule, and some of the qualities that succeed
the best may be united with grave vices or
defects; but on the whole the law is one that
cannot be questioned, and it becomes more and
more apparent as civilisation advances.

"Temperance, industry, integrity, frugality,
self-reliance, and self-restraint are the means
by which the great masses of men rise from
penury to comfort, and it is the nations in
which these qualities are most diffused that in
the long run are the most prosperous. . . .

Even the most splendid successes of life will often be found to be due much less to extraordinary intellectual gifts than to an extraordinary strength and tenacity of will, to abnormal courage, perseverance, and work-power that spring from it, or to the tact and judgment which make men skilful in seizing opportunities, and which of all intellectual qualities are most closely allied with character." [1]

Yes, character stands for most, anywhere, and in any line of business. No large house has ever been built on fraud, though some have had an origin which is not quite as clean as it might be. Still, this does not obscure the truth of the old proverb, " Honesty is the best policy." More and more people see

**Honesty as a business principle.**

that as a business principle, and apart from ethical considerations altogether, it *pays* to be honest. Success and deceptive practices are drifting farther and farther apart. The man who is bad at the heart of him, ready to take advantage of another and palm off the counterfeit for the real, may, by skilful planning, score a meteoric triumph, but, as a

[1] Lecky, *The Map of Life*, pp. 316–17.

rule, he does not remain a meteor long, and his grasping soul is not a help but a hindrance to fine achievements. Some one asks: Is, then, all commercial success founded upon strictly honest operations? We wish it were possible to answer in the affirmative. Business life is an expression of man's nature, and that is a compound of clay and Deity; consequently there are few occupations in which the clay is not in evidence. But the less there is of it the better. Whatever may be possible in the way of trade morals, there can be no doubt that the greatest scoundrel on earth appreciates the action of a debtor who pays 10s. in the pound, and, years after, the other 10s. with interest up to date. Fair dealing is not yet an impossibility —in fact, the area seems to widen—not because people are necessarily more susceptible to moral impulses, but because they find it suits their purposes better.

As to the lack of character in subordinates little need be said. The cleverest man in the world with a record for drunken- **Character and situations.** ness will have to be content to do odd jobs. What does the advertiser insinuate when he asks for copies of " recent testimonials "?

He means that character may have been good at one time, but not now. He has probably engaged a man on the strength of old letters from past employers, and found by bitter experience that a thief can show genuine documents which state he is almost a saint. Success in the service of a company, an institution, a business firm, or anywhere else, demands that a man should be trustworthy in every particular: it demands this, and much more, but character is absolutely pre-eminent. Moral delinquencies are capable of a broad interpretation. For instance, a merchant has been heard to say: " My buyer is as honest and sober as I can wish, but he does not seem to care about anything beyond routine duties —he has no enterprise. I want a man who will make *my* business *his* business." Now a

**Lack of interest a vice of character.**

lack of interest is not so serious as thieving and drunkenness, but it is serious nevertheless, and can be correctly classified as a vice of character. Such a buyer as the one described cannot hope to retain his situation long; and if he obtained it through influence, it would be another illustration of how merit inevitably comes to

the fore when a newer and better man takes
his place.  Of all limitations, lack of character
is the very worst.

Looking farther afield, we are led to see
that in regard to success a man may be handicapped by the nature of his business; in other
words, there are more opportunities of
making money in some businesses than    Some businesses more
in others.  Of course this is very obvi-    profitable
than others.
ous, but it does not receive sufficient
attention when the subject of success is dealt
with at length.  The usual cry is that any
man, in any business, at any time, can make
his fortune if he tries.  He can do nothing
of the kind.  Compare a schoolmaster with
a provision dealer.  The millionaire schoolmaster has yet to show himself on the
platform, from which he delivers an address
to an audience of pupil teachers, telling them
that they have only to work hard and they
will be millionaires like himself.  On the
other hand, the millionaire provision dealer
is quite an old acquaintance.  He may have
specialised in tea, or bacon, or sugar, but there
he is and we cannot deny him.  To the plea
that it is unfair to compare the financial results

of a professional career with those of a highly remunerative trade, we can only reply that the urging of such a plea proves the point we are seeking to establish. But let us compare two

**Draper *v.* greengrocer.** trades: a drapery store with a greengrocer's store. Given equal ability and energy in each case, it will be found that profits accumulate more rapidly with the draper than with the greengrocer: there is something in the nature of the business of the former which makes buying and selling more remunerative than in the case of the latter.

**Doctors *v.* solicitors.** Or if we compare two professions—a solicitor with a doctor—we see the same inequality. It is harder to obtain a practice as a solicitor than to obtain one as a doctor, although it is quite hard enough in both instances. A strong man, well qualified and determined to get on, will find that as a medical practitioner there are more people needing his attention than would need legal advice if he had elected to be a solicitor. Of course, circumstances alter cases, but, speaking generally, there is often a specific limitation in the nature of one's business, and this makes success, in the sense of money-getting, a thing of greater difficulty.

The same remarks apply if we compare the chances of a man in a salaried position with those of a man in business. There can be no doubt as to which one—we speak generally— has the greater possibilities before him; for, although the business man may have more care, he has few limits to hinder his development, whilst the salaried man knows within a pound or two what he will be earning **The salaried** ten years hence. True, he enjoys certain **man.** compensations in being free from worry and responsibility, but he purchases these immunities at the cost of a circumscribed activity, and even salaried positions have a tendency to involve an increasing element of trust.

Having said much on the subject of our many limitations, it will now be our pleasure to look at the other side of the question: What are our liberties? in other words, Do limitations cripple the majority of ambitious people? **Liberties and** Certainly not. Given a good physique, **limitations.** careful living, average ability, and untiring energy, and a man may succeed in almost any sphere—and with distinction, too. We can easily find excuses for comparative failure; the inventory of our limitations is generally quite up to date, and by its means we justify

our defeats without difficulty.  But how many
limits has well-directed energy?  Few indeed.
The great weakness of contemporary English
life, as a whole, is that it has so little energy
when compared with the eagerness of many
of Britain's commercial competitors.  This
arises out of a super-devotion to the world of
sport.  Business and everything else
must suffer before pastimes can be
neglected, and a trader would rather lose a
customer than miss his train for the races.
Hobbies are interesting digressions from serious pursuits, but it is not too much to say
that with an unduly large proportion of men
hobbies ultimately assume the first place, and
work degenerates into bread-and-butter routine.  We intend nothing " preachy " in these
remarks: any one with half an eye can see
these facts for himself.  The man who whines
piteously about his bad luck after having
wasted hours at chess or billiards is only
reaping what he has sown, and statesmen who are under the thumb of
diverting and distracting sport cannot be surprised if at a critical juncture they find themselves unprepared.  It is a grave matter to
speak against that sacred fetish of an English-

**The bane of
" sport."**

**Sporting
statesmen.**

man called love of sport; but when an excess
of devotion is blinding him to the claims of
commerce and citizenship, it is time to rob
him of his paltry excuses for diminishing trade
and ultra-indifference to the civic conscience.
We in this country do not suffer from a lack
of physical stamina, or paucity of brains, or
even flimsiness of character: our greatest
limitation is a lack of seriousness, the **British
insularity.** insular belief that nobody can do better
than we can, and a tendency to under-estimate
everything not labelled " English."

Energy! That is what we want. Are you
ready for hard work? the hard work of planning improvements and overcoming obstacles to
carrying them out? Are you willing to allow
a moderate margin for recreation instead of
a gospel of half work and half play? Then
rest assured there will be a day of reward.
It may not be yours to take a seat in the
highest places, or astonish the world by a
series of rapid leaps to fame and fortune; but
within your own sphere, and to some extent
beyond it, you may reap the rich reward of
industry, and the still greater reward of an
honourable name.

F

# CHAPTER VI

## WHAT IS YOUR WORK?

*" Be what Nature intended you for and you will succeed."*—SYDNEY SMITH.

THE first step towards self-realisation is self-knowledge. What is the kind of work you are best fitted to accomplish? Most men have a tendency in one specific direction, or perhaps we ought to say most *boys,* for by the time manhood has been reached the kind of work has been selected and no change is contemplated. Needless to say this selection is of the highest importance, for although there will always be a number of men who will do as well at one thing as another, the majority have definite desires in reference to the labour they prefer to take up. It is here that many **The misery of** are justified in uttering a word of com-**the misfits.** plaint. They were thrust into unsuitable occupations to satisfy a parental whim: a would-be scientist was made a shipping agent;

70

a born teacher was turned into a trader, and a born trader was compelled to figure on the Stock Exchange. Could anything be more pathetic than to behold the ruins of a great ability in a man rising up above the mediocrity of attainment in the calling to which he was obliged to submit himself? "I wanted to be an engineer," says a grocer, "but I was put to this trade instead, and here I must stick. Still, I always make a point of spending two days at the mechanical exhibitions." That man could never be a successful provision dealer. These misfits in life are a perennial source of tragedy, and although there is more than a touch of humour in seeing a born poet analysing invoices and bills of lading at a roll-top desk, the pitiableness of it all is unspeakable. Once the right man gets into the wrong place it requires infinite trouble to get him out again.

But how shall the right place be found? Can a youth in his teens decide the issue with a just estimate of his own powers? Much depends on the youth himself, but, generally speaking, he will follow his strongest desires, and his strongest desires

*Finding the right place.*

arise out of the exercise of the faculty which is strongest in him. " Pope wrote excellent verses at fourteen. Pascal composed at sixteen a tractate on the conic sections. Nelson made up his mind to be a hero before he was old enough to be a midshipman, and Bacon busied himself with the defects of Aristotle when he was fifteen." Nowadays parents ask: " What shall we do with our boys? " That does not sound as if the boys were going to have much to do with the matter. Parents who want " a clergyman in the family," or who would " so like one of the sons to be a doctor," little know what this pressure means to a boy who wishes to please his parents even at the expense of following his own inclinations. Moreover, the professions are quite crowded enough already, and genteel poverty needs no further additions to its ranks. In olden times children were made to pass through the fires of Moloch, **Parental vanities.** and fathers and mothers no doubt felt very cheerful when their consciences were satisfied by this painful spectacle. In these days we have lost the barbarity, but the sacrifice still continues, and sons are placed in positions which will tickle parental vanity and feed its inordinate ambition. No; the question is not: " What shall we do with our boys? " but: " What can they do for themselves, and how can we help them? "

The smart youth in his teens should be told that the time has arrived when he must draw a map of life. At first he will probably treat the subject as we all did **Forming a** at his age, and make it the butt of tea- **decision.** table jokes; but the season of unbecoming levity will pass away and give place to serious thought, with the result that a definite plan is made, and real work commences in earnest. Probably the choice is one that was expected, for the natural bent of the mind is generally apparent; but if the choice comes as a surprise and turns out to be a trade and not a profession, it will be the height of folly to satirise the suggested course in the hope of its being abandoned. Besides, why should it be abandoned? Why should trade be stigmatised in the least possible degree? By-and-by trade pursuits will have cap- **Trades v.** tured the best brains available. Not **professions.** long ago the president of an American university, in lamenting the dearth of capable teachers, said: " I have concluded, and the conclusion saddens me, that most youths of ~~force prefer commercial careers. The stronger~~ boys go into business, or into the active professions." The commercial spirit is not so far developed in England as in America or Germany, but there is a perceptible move- ment in that direction. The growing enthu- siasm for higher business education, and the granting of commercial degrees by our lead- ing universities, are indicative of the right feeling.

At this juncture we shall be met by the **An objection.** old objections, namely, that youths often show no particular bent for any kind of occu- pation, or, if they make a selection at all, they do so from whim or passing fancy. For instance, there is the youth who wants to go to sea. He will hear of nothing else. Very well, let him go; and if his optimism survives the first voyage it is more than likely that he has hit upon the life for which he is best suited; but if not, it only means that he must once more face the question at the head of this chapter, " What is your work? " Not

three out of six find their proper habitat at
the first seeking, and the youth who exhibits
no special predilection, as well as the dis-
illusioned sailor-boy, must try again, **Seeking and**
and still again, until they discover a **finding.**
congenial environment. Doubtless, this
" changing about " has serious disadvantages,
but hardly so serious as those which follow
a wrong-headed devotion to a round of duties
that become positively loathsome, for under
such conditions success is out of the question;
but once the happier sphere is found, the
possibilities of expansion begin to open out.

It is surprising to know how many young
fellows on both sides of twenty are **Round men in**
round men in square holes. Poverty, **square holes.**
chance, family affairs, and a host of other
circumstances are the alleged causes of this
state of things, but the cause is a detail compared with the consequence. How are these
men to find the right work? Well, experience
and observation have told them where they
will be more successful: what is now needed
is a strenuous and sustained effort to get there,
and that of course rests entirely with the man.
The youth who was suddenly called upon to

take up his father's uncongenial business in
order to keep the family together is to be
commended for filial duty and self-sacrifice,
but so soon as the years of drudgery are over,
and he is free to follow his own inclinations,
he must take the measure of his powers (if he
has not previously) and then seek diligently
for an opportunity. In other words, he must
find his own work: no one will take special
trouble to find it for him. Mr. E. W.
Bok, who, having succeeded himself,
can speak as an authority on these points,
says: "Every man is given a certain thing to
do in the world, and he alone, by a proper
study of himself, can arrive at the clearest
and surest knowledge of that particular object.
I am a firm believer in the moulding of character through the influence of another; but
my conviction is equally strong that every man
is the architect of his own fortune, and that
his truest course in life is to follow, not the
guidance of another, but his own instincts.
In other words, I think young men should, as
early in life as possible, get into touch with
the idea of their own responsibility, and be
taught the great lesson that, however well

*An American editor's view.*

others may advise, they, and they alone, must carve out their own careers. The most successful careers, the most honourable lives in the history of the world, are those which have been shaped by their own hands. There is an element of danger in this, of course, but the element is small in comparison with the greater danger which lies in the foundation of a character against one's own instincts."

A man who does not believe in himself sufficiently to strike out an individual course and follow his own conclusions **Know yourself to trust yourself.** must be written down as a failure. Self-reliance and self-knowledge go together. But, it will be asked, how can a man get to know himself? Must he squat on the ground like a Hindu, and, directing his vision to the tip of his nose, repeat that blessed word *ôm?* No, it is much simpler than that. A phrenologist is said to reveal a man to himself—his laziness, lack of energy, or his want of principle—but let a man act as his own phrenologist, not by examining his bumps so much as observing his habits and analysing his tastes, and he will soon be able to know what he can do and what he cannot.

# CHAPTER VII

## ORIGINALITY: THE KEY

*" New, daring, and inspiring ideas are engendered only in a clear head over a glowing heart."*—F. JACOBS.

THERE is only one key to open the door of notable prosperity, and that is the key of originality. Now originality is one of those words about which we often dispute among ourselves, and before we can attach a definite meaning to it in this chapter, we shall have to inquire into its uses in other connections. A **Originality** popular dictionary defines it as follows: **defined.** " The power of originating new thoughts or uncommon combinations of thoughts." That sounds as if the definition had been coined in the interests of literature alone, but it is not so. Originality connotes just what our dictionary says, for a man may be able to originate new thoughts and not be able to express them, either in literature or mechanical inventions. Nevertheless, the word

itself has been so closely identified with literature that a man must veritably startle the world
before he can rejoice in the appellation "original," and yet, as a matter of fact, if he has
put brains into business, and if he conducts it
on lines which he has thought out for himself,
he is actually an original man, even though the
newspapers never heard of him.

Let us take two illustrations, one from literature and one from business. Shakespeare,
Walter Scott, and George Eliot are representa-
tives of great names in literary invention, **Originality in**
and in regard to originality they enjoy **literature.**
distinctive fame. But they do not enjoy it in
the same degree. George Eliot is not so
original as Walter Scott, and Walter Scott
is not so original as Shakespeare, and yet
each of the three is an original writer express-
ing "new thoughts or uncommon combinations
of thoughts." Of course this fact is obvious
enough, but we restate it in order to emphasise
a protest against the too common practice of
marking off literary originality with almost
scientific exactness. From Shakespeare down to
the meanest minor poet who achieves one good
line in fifty the question is entirely one of degree.

In commercial matters it is the same—only
the pay is greater.  For instance, there is the
originality of Sir Henry Bessemer, who in-
vented the Bessemer process for making steel.

**Originality in business.** That process required very considerable
scientific knowledge and much patient
investigation, but the reward in fame and
wealth was ample compensation for the labour
spent in experiments.  Sir George Newnes
may be taken as exhibiting another kind of
originality in the realm of press enterprises,
but both men possessed the power of discovery—one in chemical processes, the other
in public needs.  It is a far cry from enterprise of this kind to the more mechanical originality of the clock manufacturer whose chief
aim was to keep his wares before the people.
His method was to add a new cog, or remodel
the case, or paint the face in a new way, or
do something else equally trifling, and then
blazon forth these changes in the public prints.
By this artifice he created a ready market for
his goods, although no step was taken in the
invention of a new principle or the improvement of an old one.

It is plain, therefore, that there is as much

difference between the originality of Sir Henry Bessemer and the tricky clockmaker in business, as there is between Shakespeare and a minor poet in literature.   As for origin- **A question** ality itself, it is far easier of attainment **of degree.** in business than in literature.   If a merchant spent half as much time over writing an advertisement on new lines as a poet does over a single word in a single line, we should not have to admit the necessity for the commercial warcry of " England! Wake up "; for the exhibition of intense earnestness, thus displayed, would augur well for the discovery of a thousand originalities.

It is the same everywhere; let the business be making matches or making an empire, creating poems, or creating industries, serving behind the counter or serving the State —the original man, the thinker, always wins. There would be fewer so-called failures if this fact were better understood, for many a hard worker, following old and playedout methods, cannot for the life of him see why " slogging away " seems to accomplish so little.   The world waits for men with new ideas.

But how is a man to be original if there be no originality in him? Well, that is a hard question—or an easy one—whichever way we choose to look at it. For instance, we might say: " A man has an original cast of mind or he has not. If he has, it will manifest itself unmistakably; if he has not, he may think until Doomsday, but he will never give birth to an original idea; or, if he does, the chances are that he has no practical talent to use it to advantage." An answer of this description is easy to give, because one is spared the trouble of analysing facts which seem to point the other way. That is where the real difficulty comes in; for, in business, there are scores who have succeeded, not only by dint of hard work, but by striking out on new lines, who cannot easily be called men of original minds. The history of inventions seems to teach that pertinacity of attention to particular problems on the part of men of average capacity has produced surprising results. Naturally, the clever man's concentration will produce greater results than that of less gifted individuals, but in the long run the persistent man with ordinary brains

*Can originality be developed?*

*What concentration can do.*

achieves, comparatively speaking, positions of greater distinction.   The truly original man can perhaps discover a new way of making money after five minutes' reflection, and in a week is ready for action.   But there is no reason why an average man, by close attention, should not arrive at the same result in five months' time.   This would not make him an original man in the usual sense, but nevertheless he would accomplish by " long patience " what comes to the other man almost intuitively.   Draw up a list of the successful men you know in finance, in trade, in the professions.   What kind of men are they?   Men, in most cases, with one idea.   Aye, there's the secret of it all.   They chose their sub-   **Men with** ject, and read, thought, and dreamed   **one idea.** of nothing else.   Concentration will explain more than two-thirds of commercial originality, whatever it may do in literature.

But, it will be asked, why is originality the key to success?   Because the old ways have too many adherents already, and rapid progress is easiest where there is least competition.   People want businesses which pay large profits, and it follows as a consequence that the more people engage in such businesses, the less the profits will become.

New businesses and large profits.

So, in turn, every new line becomes an old line, and its remunerativeness decreases. "Nothing is more certain than that when a business pays very large profits its race is nearly run. Those who are already in it may get rich, but the late comers, who strike in only after its profitableness has leaked out and become known to the whole community, will . . . cut down the profits to a point so fine as to render them merely nominal or worse." Fortune smiles on those who are the first to discover and supply some new want of society, some new source of profit, or some speciality that is popular with the masses of the people. These discoverers are original men of the first order, but there is room for originality even in the established lines of business. "Let every man stick

Develop your own work.

to the business he knows, constantly studying new plans to make it more productive, to lessen his expenses, and to increase his profits. The man who knows all about a ship from the keel up will make a living profit, while the amateur, who only knows what others tell him, will lose. The foreign trader, who knows precisely the wants of the market to which he sends his goods, will get rich, while his neighbour, who gets his information at second hand from prices current, and general information accessible to everybody, will inevitably fail."

G

# CHAPTER VIII

## HOW SOME MEN HAVE SUCCEEDED

*" Biography is the only true history."*

CARLYLE.

IN this chapter we propose to deal with those motive powers to action, and those qualities of mind and character, which go to explain the success of a certain number of men with whose names we are familiar. The method will be twofold. We shall first allow the successful man to interpret himself, and then we shall try to see how far his interpretation agrees with our own view.

I. We are indebted to *The Young Man* for the following opinions. They represent the ideas of the practical man.

(*a*) ALDERMAN SIR W. P. TRELOAR.—

Sir W. P. Treloar. "My advice is . . . work hard, and take an interest in your work. Merely working hard as a machine will not do; an interest must be taken in the work, an individuality must be shown.

"How often one hears it said: 'Oh, I have not a very good memory; I do not remember all the small details of the matter, but the general purport was so and so.' The young man who talks like that has not taken sufficient interest in the matter to remember the details. Hear him speak of something else in which he does take an interest; his memory then is so good that he forgets nothing. I have known some of the most successful business men in London, and have always been struck by their thorough knowledge of all the details of any business matter they are connected with. It is said of them: 'What good memories they have!' which means they have taken an interest in matters of business which come before them."

(b) SIR RICHARD TANGYE.—"One great secret of the success that has been given me is, undoubtedly, the life-long habit I have had of giving close attention to small details. Nothing has been too small to receive my attention. Things that most young people seem to think are really too trifling, and which they resent having their notice drawn to, have never been too small for me. I often think that the human race is divided mainly into two classes—those who attend to small details (such as closing the doors behind them, and tipping up the basin in the lavatory), and those who don't.

"It is of course very much easier for an energetic person to do a multitude of little things than to ask his young people to do them, although they pertain to them-selves; but when a man has a number of children, or is much in contact with young people, it is often quite as much his duty *not* to do a thing as it is theirs to do it. And **Details.** so, often feeling that I shall be con-sidered churlish or cranky, I, for the hundredth time, call their attention to what they think 'small things' (generally ending by doing them myself), feeling that I am responsible for their training, and that it may 'come to them,' although perhaps after many days. If young men could only realise what an in-fluence attention to 'little things' has upon the formation of character, and of what im-portance the formation of character in youth is, they would never despise 'the day of small things.'

"During a very busy life I have often been asked, 'How do you manage to do it all?' The answer is very simple: it is because I do everything *promptly*. Procrastination . . . is fatal. To-morrow has always duties of its own to be attended to. The young man in the parable said, 'I go, sir,' and went not. It is very likely he intended to go all the while, but put it off and then forgot all about it. When I was a boy I had a companion who often accompanied me to school—or, rather, he kept twenty yards behind me; and in response to calls to 'Come on,' would reply, 'Stop a bit.' That characteristic has stuck to him all through life. . . . And so, to sum up the whole matter, I would say, 'Whatsoever thy hand findeth to do, do it with all thy might,' and 'Do it at once.'"

(c) WALTER HAZELL, M.P.—"'How to Succeed in Business' is a difficult subject to write upon. There is no royal road to success. Some attain it by promptly using any accidental opportunity, while others, perhaps more deserving, are unsuccessful through

*Walter Hazell.*

circumstances entirely beyond their control. In general, I believe that ability, united with great industry and unswerving perseverance, ultimately get their reward. The capacity to develop improved methods of production or distribution benefits alike the inventor and the entire community. It is more satisfactory to pursue steady industry than to seek success by a short cut; but beware of keeping slavishly in old ruts. A good reputation carefully built up and steadily maintained is an immense advantage. A particular calling may be depressed through temporary circumstances, such as supply being greater than demand, but this need not deter a young man from entering it, because, unless it is a dying industry, things right themselves in the course of time. Another calling may be remarkably prosperous, but before the novice can get established in it the rush of competitors has ruined his fair prospects.

"Success in business means failure in life if it be gained by unworthy practices; while the humble home and the small income are success indeed if they are chosen instead of dishonourable roads to an enormous fortune."

(*d*) JOHN MORGAN RICHARDS.—"I should
say that remarkable genius, endowment, **John Morgan**
or 'good luck' have very little to do **Richards.**
with business success, but that great industry,
close application, punctuality, honesty, indom-
itable perseverance, and what the author of
*John Halifax, Gentleman*, called 'being
dependable,' would make for success always.
I can most certainly say that in my experience
and observation I have not known these
qualities to fail, and that those who possess
them are called successful."

(*e*) SIR GEORGE NEWNES, Bart.—"Let a
man take as much interest in his work **Sir G. Newnes.**
as he does in his pleasures and he will succeed
in business."

(*f*) ALDERMAN EVAN SPICER.—"I would
say to all young men who wish to suc- **Ald. E. Spicer.**
ceed in business in the highest sense, 'Go
straight, help others, and aim at being the
Christian gentleman.'"

(*g*) SIR PHILIP MANFIELD.—"To a man
wishing to rise in the world, Smiles **Sir Philip**
says: 'Always do your best; if you **Manfield.**
want to get on, you must put your shoulder
to the wheel.' Do not be afraid of work; and

remember that, whatever you owe to others, it is a duty you owe to yourself to succeed in your undertakings. Be careful of your character; it is the principal capital of the young tradesman. Do not put off the duties of to-day; to-morrow will bring its own burdens. Be just in your dealings with those you serve, and considerate to those who are serving you. Keep your business accounts with scrupulous exactness, and your private expenditure with great care and watchfulness, and do not lose sight of your duty to your poorer brethren. Do not be cast down by any temporary difficulty; to-morrow may clear away the cloud. Be careful in the choice of your associates; there is an old proverb, ' Show me the company a man keeps, and I will tell you what manner of man he is.' Take care of your health; the rules for guidance are simple. . . . Take every opportunity of cultivating your higher faculties; when the time of leisure comes have some resources worthy of your position. ' Man shall not live by bread alone.' "

(*h*) Mr. C. MOBERLY BELL, Manager of the *Times*.—" On entering business: (1) Don't

regard too much your pay.   It is the height of
the ladder and not the height of the first      Mr. C.
rung that is important; (2) When you      Moberly Bell.
know thoroughly your own work, try to master
that of the man above you; (3) If your business
is only to sweep a crossing, remember that it
is your business to make that the best swept
crossing in the world."

(*i*) SIR WILLIAM DUNN.—" You must give
close application to business if you ex-      Sir Wm.
pect to be successful.  Punctuality, steadi-      Dunn.
ness, reliability, and strict attention to detail
are invaluable virtues, but in addition to these a
knowledge of human character is indispensable.
You must know whom to trust and whom to
guard against. In all your dealings be absolutely
honest.  Never try to overreach any one.  Let
people feel sure that you will stand by your word,
and treat them in a straightforward manner,
and you will win their confidence and custom."

(*j*) SIR JAMES RECKITT, Bart.—" In both
buying and selling, do unto others as      Sir J. Reckitt.
you would be done by.  Be civil to all men,
and take especial pains to accommodate your
customers in what they require, provided it
leave sufficient profit.  Don't advertise your

wares unless you sell of the best, or have really some improvement to offer upon what has hitherto been in use."

(*k*) Sir T. J. Lipton, Bart.—" To young men I would say that the moulding of their future lives is in their own hands. They often get opportunities for advancement, but do not embrace them. If, however, they start with a definite object in view, determined to work hard, take an intelligent interest in their duties, not make too much of a bargain about long hours, and do to others as they would like to be done by, there is no fear but that they will succeed—they are bound to have success."

Sir T. J. Lipton.

(*l*) Mr. J. S. Fry.—" I believe that success in life depends more upon character and industry than upon great natural ability or talent. Many young men think they can achieve sudden success by some fortunate circumstance, but as a rule it has to be reached by persevering industry and hard work. There should be a determination to do everything— even in the humblest position—in the best possible way, rather than a restless anxiety to do something else which may seem more desirable. Promotion will come in due time.

Mr. J. S. Fry.

I lay great stress on reliability. If a young man can always be depended upon, he is almost certain to be valued. . . . "

(*m*) T. H. W. IDRIS, L.C.C.—"In my opinion success in business is dependent  **T. H. W. Idris.** on three things: (1) Spend less than you earn; (2) Take care that your business is done in the best and most honest manner in every detail; (3) Let your principal desire be to work your business well, and in such a way as to be beneficial to yourself and those who are dependent on you, or to those who have claims upon you, and to the community. These three points may be elaborated considerably. No. 1 involves, of course, business calculation—as self-denial and careful calculation are absolutely indispensable to success. No. 2 involves the application of the maxim, 'Honesty is the best policy,' pursued from the highest motive. It also involves supplying the best article in your line of business. No. 3 involves fair treatment of all those who are engaged with you in business, in order to obtain their hearty co-operation, and the distribution of a good share of the financial results in an unselfish manner.

(*n*) MR. C. ARTHUR PEARSON.—" First, and to my mind most important of all, embark on a business which suits you. I believe that there are thousands of business men who are, comparatively speaking, failures, simply because they went into businesses which do not interest them in the least. If your work does not interest you it is perfectly impossible to do your best at it. On the other hand, work in which you feel a keen interest ceases to be work in the ordinary acceptance of the term. . . . When I was eighteen I very nearly became a bank clerk. I am convinced that I should have been a dismal failure at a bank counter, simply because my work would have had no interest for me whatever. That I have not been a failure at my business is, I am sure, chiefly because I take the keenest interest in it.

Mr. C. A. Pearson.

" And when you have decided what business interests you, stick to it like a limpet. Get up with it in the morning, and go to bed with it at night. Think about it all the time. Then if you have average intelligence, you are bound to succeed, and success will bring leisure in which to enjoy it. But don't try to take your leisure until you have secured your success."

(*o*) MR. THOMAS SMITH.—"As one who has risen from the bottom rung of the lad- **Mr. T. Smith.** der, I attribute my present great success primarily to the fear of God, which I received as a young man; and secondarily, to my steadfast adherence to temperance principles.    Prayer, the study of God's Word, a reverence for the Sabbath, strict integrity in business, strong sympathy for young men and child life, promptitude in meeting engagements, a habit of always keeping work well in hand, ever looking ahead for new opportunities of usefulness, and perhaps most of all, while not over anxious for fresh talents, using with diligence the experience gained all along the line of life—these are all helps to success."

II. In critically examining these confessions —for such indeed they are—the first remark to be made is that they are modern.    Most of the contributors—if not all—are still actively engaged in business life.    This is a great advantage in adding interest and in- **Value of** struction to the present chapter.    One **modern** grows a little tired of hearing about **examples.** George Stephenson, Samuel Budgett, and a host of others who have "risen."    They were

good men, but, having received repeated bio-
graphical notice, it is time we allowed them
to rest.    There are men nearer to our own
day and generation who are quite as worthy
of our regard.    Besides, there is a disposition
to argue that the earlier men had an easier
way to fame and fortune than the men of
to-day.    We need therefore to bring the biography of success up to date in order to make
the reader—the young reader especially—
feel that whatever difference period may cause
in the scope of opportunity, there is a con-
tinuous history of commercial achievements.

Among the contributors to the symposium
we notice a few minor differences, but no more
than were to be expected.    Sir Richard Tangye
is a little too emphatic on " details," and the
illustrations he gives do not help him, as they
refer to personal tidiness rather than to " details " as important elements in business practice.    Some successful men abhor details
(notably the late Cecil J. Rhodes) ; not that
they despise them, but they prefer to leave the
**Words in** " fag " of arranging them to others.    Mr.
**criticism.** Fry would appear to emphasise reliability too much.    We have known employees as

reliable as the laws of Nature, but they never achieved anything in the way of distinctive success, although they waited long for the day of promotion; it suited their masters' pockets best to keep them where they were. For a salaried man the three points indicated by Mr. Moberly Bell are excellent.

On comparing the contributions to see how far they agree in ascribing success to one factor pre-eminently, we see at once that they all urge a plea for *vital interest in one's work*. Mr. C. A. Pearson wisely pro- **Vital interest the motive power.** vides for a kind of work in which it is possible to take an interest, but no one urges the plea more strongly than he. There is nothing about luck being a serious question to face; "influence" as a feature of progress is hardly so much as mentioned; and even originality does not figure to any appreciable extent. This would seem to militate against the whole argument of a previous chapter, but it is only seeming, not real. *Vital interest* is the dynamic power which sets in action all the faculties of man; it causes him to seek the best and most economical means to accomplish a desired end; it shows him the advantage of husbanding resources and exercising care in expenditure; it starts new trains of thought, opens out new vistas of enterprise, and turns drudgery into pleasure; indeed, there is no point, no fact, no action on which it has not a direct bearing.

Whatever you do, therefore, you must take a deep interest in your work.  This is the dictum of every successful man everywhere. Read *Men of Achievement,* which deals with prominent commercial magnates in the United **American** States, and you will find the same pro- **testimony.** nouncements.    Marshall Field, G. M. Pullman, P. D. Armour, C. W. Field, and L. P. Morton—they all say the same thing: *enthusiasm, interest, determination.*

# CHAPTER IX

## QUESTIONS AND ANSWERS

*" He that questioneth much will learn much."*—BACON.

(1) *How much has influence to do with success, and does not the absence of this power account for many failures?*

THIS is a general question, and must receive a general answer. Influence can put a man into a prominent position, but it cannot make a success of him; it can give numerous chances, and offer many advantages, but it cannot change the man himself. Take military promotions as an illustration. An officer with social and political powers behind his ambitions is pushed ahead of others who are more deserving from the standpoint of ability. What happens? As a rule nothing striking in any way. The promoted man draws his pay and enjoys it; the worthier candidate for honours has to be content with

**Army influ-ence.**

his smaller allowance—and wait.    That is
how the military world wags, not sometimes,
but too often.    But when promoted inefficiency
has to take to the battlefield, and fight an
enemy that hides itself as in the Boer war—
how then?    It is just the same in business.
Let influence give a managership to a man
who has no aptitude for controlling others, or
a secretaryship to a youth who is devoid of
the correspondence instinct, and a ghastly
failure in each case will be the result.    Influence is of no service to the incompetent, but
to a good man it is an immense help.    Nowadays one hears influence spoken of as if it
were gone out of fashion.    It will never go
out of fashion so long as society remains on
its present basis, and special prerogatives

**Influence still**    are granted to men on account of their
**powerful.**    position.    Neither will influence go out
of fashion as long as commerce is conducted
on non-socialistic lines; for in trade operations
the man of wealth wields the same influence
as the man of social distinction in another
sphere.    A clever man, with strong friends
behind him, can never be equalled by another
man of like ability, but destitute of helpful

friendships and all the little items which go to give him a " pull."   On the other hand, no man need fail because these elements of success are absent; indeed, prevailing sentiment is so much in favour of progress by merit alone, that there is a disposition to deny the power of influence altogether.   If " influence " can be dispensed with, a man will probably feel more satisfied with himself; but there is no reason why he should despise helps of various kinds, provided he loses nothing in manliness by accepting the assistance they offer.

(2) *How far is lack of education responsible for inability to succeed?*

It all depends on the meaning attached to the word " education."   In some cases the presence of education is responsible for failure, in other cases its absence is the real secret of success. If a man can neither read nor write, he labours under severe disadvantages; but even **In spite of** then he has frequently been known to **education.** rise above them, and attain to wealth and position, the curious feature of the case being that a sense of limitation begot a greater

determination to succeed. Education, beyond
the three R's, as it is pursued to-day, does
not seem, except in technical matters, to add
to the power of making a living; its contribu-
tion is offered too exclusively to the *ideal* side
of our nature and too little to the *real*. But

**The cry for utility.** the utilitarian spirit is winning everywhere. At one time it would have been
a crime to allow a man to obtain a university
degree without a fair knowledge of Latin, but
in the University of London this is now possible. Latin used to be, and indeed continues
to be, in many quarters, one of the necessary
foundations of a liberal education, and Lord
Goschen, commercially minded as he is, still
argues in favour of classical studies for youths
who will enter business. The older concep-
tions are, however, slowly but surely changing.
Scholarship has been too closely identified
with one particular curriculum which was considered an end in itself. Nowadays men—
unashamed—are asking, " What education is
most *useful* for my sons and daughters?"

As yet the true utilitarian method has not
been practically realised. Too much attention
is given to specific subjects, too little to the

cultivation of mental power.   To succeed in
any department of life one must know certain
things and know them well, but the greatest
requisites of all are a trained mind and a
tutored eye.   This is why so many men,
uneducated in the accepted sense of the term,
achieve successes of considerable magnitude.
A course of academical training would have
turned their attention to other pursuits, and
filled their minds with other ideals than those
which were eventually accepted; and it would
have exerted a tendency to fit them into the
common mould of men instead of allowing individuality to have full play.   We need education, but it must be of the right kind.   It
must quicken the perceptions, sensuous and
mental; it must teach the mind how to
think, how to analyse and how to decide; it must tutor the memory and
link together all facts by the laws of association.   The school of experience will teach
much of this curriculum, but that is no reason
why the school of earlier years should follow
a system which wastes precious time and
renders the way more difficult; it is all the
more reason why the system should model its

The requi-
sites of edu-
cation.

actions on what will be required when life begins in earnest.

If, then, a man can read and write, and is able to work such arithmetical problems as are common to all kinds of commercial transactions, with accuracy and despatch—in a word, if he be an English scholar—there is really nothing to keep him back; but if he spells accommodate with one " m," and disappointment with two " s's," and is never certain of his figures, he labours under serious disadvantages, and ought to remove them as early as possible. Even then it is only fair to say that the ranks of successful men include a number who would not shine either in penmanship, or orthography, or calculations in the technical sense—shortcomings which they lament more than any one else, but which— to their honour be it said—they have nobly surmounted by sheer industry and native intelligence.

In those pursuits where scientific or other technical knowledge is an absolute necessity, it is of course obvious that the uneducated man has no chance whatever. Brain power is of no avail apart

*Where education is a necessity.*

from training and experience. The foreign correspondent must know his languages, the engineer his strains and resistances, the barrister his law, and the doctor his medicine.

(3) *Is not the possession of capital one of the great secrets of success?*

Yes and No. If Mr. Pierpont Morgan had not inherited capital, it might be that he would not have figured so significantly in the world's commerce as he has done; or it might be otherwise. That the possession of capital to the right kind of man is an immense **Where capital** advantage goes without saying; and **is a gain.** if the right kind of man is minus capital, it stands to reason that his progress will be infinitely slower than in the case of a more favoured rival. Capital is a secret of success in the sense of providing rapid means for its attainment. Money makes money. Cecil Rhodes started as a dreamer, but he soon realised that big ideas were nothing unless he had money to carry them into execution. He therefore sought capital as a means to an end.

But he started as the right kind of man

minus—the needful.   Most of the great names
in commerce must be included in the same
category; for, as a rule, where capital
has not to be sought, a man fails to
find the impulse towards struggle and achievement; he is disposed to rest on his oars, or
else dabble in a few things to keep his mind
occupied.   True, there are brilliant exceptions, but this is the general rule; and it
shows that the possession of capital is more
often than not a secret of lethargy and commercial somnolence.

**Where it is a loss.**

(4) *What is to be said of the use of business
maxims?*

Maxims are like Carlyle's definition of pro-
verbs: " short sentences from long experience."   Some are good, some are bad, others
are indifferent.   Everything depends on the
maxim-maker.   We can safely say that " if
industry comes in at the door, poverty
flies out through the window," but we do
not readily assent to the saying, " Never
borrow; never lend."   We know what
the intention is, but these arbitrary pro-

**Maxims criticised.**

hibitives, which only see white and black in life — no shadings — are based on wooden Puritanism. " Take care of the pence and the pounds will take care of themselves," is a maxim of gentler calibre, but none the less liable to misapplication. " Judicious expenditure has probably made more fortunes than saving and economy have; and even among those whose incomes are not large, and whose resources are limited (clerks in banks and similar institutions, men in business, or budding professional men), the expenditure of a disproportionately large part of income on appearances is frequently one of the very best investments that could be made with the money." [1]   In other words, niggardliness over pence is not to-day a paying policy.

Most men have what are called " favourite virtues," and in speaking of the conditions of success they are sure to give undue **Favourite** emphasis to those qualities which **virtues.** appeal to them more strongly than others. Thus of the two maxims, " Be a teetotaler " and " Keep out of debt," one will be selected

[1] *Luck, Merit and Success* (*Nat. Rev.*, vol. xvii., 1891).

—the one which has been seen in its best type of obedience and in its most miserable specimens of disobedience. Mr. Carnegie may not ~~have seen hideous pictures of what a~~ small debt can lead to, but he has witnessed the colossal effects of alcohol, and does not hesitate to give teetotalism a first place in his list of maxims. We should be churlish indeed to utter a word of protest against any one who sought to warn men of the dangers that lurk in the absurd drinking habits of the day—habits which are, in too many instances, degrading in themselves even when they do **Drink and** not directly incapacitate. Still, we have **debt.** quite as much to do with money as we have with drink, and we have a right to ask that the maxim-maker shall coin a convenient phrase to help us in the one as in the other. What the individual observer finds to be most important is not the true criterion; it is what the world requires as a whole, and the money-conscience needs as much prominence as the preaching of total abstinence. As a collection of practical maxims, those attributed to Baron Rothschild are worthy of careful study. Here is the list :—

Attend carefully to the details of your business.

Be prompt in all things.

Consider well, then decide positively.

Dare to do right; fear to do wrong.

**Baron Roth-child's maxims.**

Endure trials patiently.

Fight life's battles bravely, manfully.

Go not into the society of the vicious.

Hold integrity sacred.

Injure not another's reputation or business.

Join hands only with the virtuous.

Keep your mind from evil thoughts.

Lie not for any consideration.

Make few acquaintances.

Never try to appear what you are not.

Observe good manners.

Pay your debts promptly.

Question not the veracity of a friend.

Respect the counsel of your parents.

Sacrifice money rather than principle.

Touch not, taste not, handle not intoxicating drinks.

Use your leisure time for improvement.

'Xtend to every one a kindly salutation.

Yield not to discouragement.

Zealously labour for the right and success is certain.

There is an amount of repetition in the
twenty-four maxims, due largely to the artificial form in which they are cast—A to Z—
but, on the whole, they embody a good deal
of sound practical wisdom. Naturally, something depends on the way we interpret
a rule of conduct, and the method we
adopt to translate it into action. Take the
following, " Make few acquaintances." That
sounds somewhat irrational. Provided we
make good acquaintances—pleasant socially
and helpful commercially—why not make a
good many? If the Baron meant evil acquaintances, why did he not say so? Probably
he had in mind the enormous waste of time
that goes on in social functions of all kinds,
functions that are prolonged into the early
hours, and which sap the life and spirit of a
man as well as drain his financial resources.
Who would not, with any sense at all, make
few acquaintances if this was to be the result
of making many?

If we should attempt to supplement the list
we might advantageously suggest the
inclusion of a sentence urging the
reader to keep clear of legal squabbles as far

**The maxims analysed.**

**Avoid legal strife.**

as possible. Never go to law unless you are compelled to do so. No word need be spoken against professional men who are honest and true, but the system of legal procedure is such that, even with a good case and a winning verdict, you may leave the Court all the worse and none the better. Either as plaintiff or defendant, you stand for a target to a cross-examining barrister, who has perfect liberty to soil an unsullied reputation by ventilating insinuations which have not a shadow of truth.

For a business man, however, there is one maxim which, like charity, covers a multitude of sins: it is summed up tersely **Pay up!** though somewhat vulgarly in the colloquialism: " Pay up! "

A man may be very far gone morally, but if he pays up his debts promptly he nearly scores off the bad marks against him. We hear people say: " He's an awful blackguard, and he treats his family shamefully, but he always sends in his money to the minute." We may not agree with these moral judgments which put "cash down " in one scale and a pile of iniquities in the other, making an equal balance; but there is no business man who is indisposed to give a very high place to the merit of prompt remittances; and as a maxim of far-reaching effects, mental and moral, " Pay up " certainly ought to be one of the first to receive the ambitious youth's attention.

(5) *Are there not many instances of deserving men who completely fail in the attempt to succeed?*

Certainly; merit too often has to lie low whilst pushful mediocrity scores its triumph. The reason is a simple one: *merit must be marketable.* A beautiful character is not directly a commercial commodity; it will not **A market** of itself buy a dinner or purchase a **for merit.** night's rest: money or labour alone can do that. Hence, if a man has no money, or is unable to perform any kind of labour to earn money, he soon begins to starve. Approach the question from another point of view by asking, " What is a deserving man? " Generally he is steady and sober, even industrious, but he lacks a knowledge of how to use his abilities to the best worldly advantage, or else he lacks altogether the powers that make for earning a living. This is equivalent to saying

that he is not receiving from the world all that
is due to him as an upright man and an honest
citizen.    But the world never professes to
dispense its benefits on moral principles by
giving wealth and fame to the pure in heart.
The pure in heart have a reward all their
own, but earthly rewards are the direct     Earthly re-
result of pursuing earthly things in ac-     wards by
cordance with earthly methods.   Conse-     earthly
methods.
quently, however deserving a man may be in
moral and religious character, if he lives in
the world and is not of it, he can hardly expect to reap the world's reward.   This is why
so many men of good character fail dismally.

Again, the man whose vocation lies on the
ideal side of life, and who possesses commen-
surate mental culture, frequently feels that his
labours do not meet with the reward they
deserve.   True, but again we say merit must
be marketable.   It will take more time to
learn, and write a comparative grammar of,
European languages than it will to write a
passable novel, and yet the chances are     Philologian
that the novelist will make money whilst     versus
Novelist.
the philologian merely earns a pittance.
There is a greater market for stories than for

comparative grammars, and the philologian must suffer accordingly. As a rule, however, the idealist of all types never pretends to compete with others on trade lines, and, although dissatisfied with his own financial receipts, consoles himself with the reflection that at least he has gained some small share of worldly distinction. In no sense except the money sense is he an unsuccessful man.

Deserving men, either from the standpoint of character or mental ability, or both, fail, in nine cases out of ten, through some defect in the capacity for action: they do not know what to do, or how to do it, or else they are ever bungling. We have read somewhere of a philosopher who engaged a ferryman to row him across a Highland lake. A storm came on, and the waves splashed into the boat. "Do you understand ontology?" said the philosopher; and on receiving a reply in the negative, he said, "Then, boatman, you have lost *half* your existence." The boat began to toss dangerously, and the ferryman said, "Can you swim, sir?" "No," was the response. "Then you have lost *the whole* of

**Defect in capacity for action.**

**The half and the whole.**

your existence, for this boat will be under water in two minutes."

The philosopher was a man of thought, but in a storm even ability to understand Hegel would not keep his head above water; whilst the ferryman, who never cared a straw whether he knew ontology or not, would quickly swim ashore.

But what about the one man in ten, who, though deserving, was a failure, and whose failure could not be explained on the line of impracticality? To this question we have no reply to offer. There is a mystery in the lives of some men and women that no known philosophy can explain. They have character, ability, and determination — but for some occult reason they never get on. Possibly if the tangled web of their life were unravelled, we should see where the mistakes had been made; but, so far as human knowledge can decide, these unfortunate people will remain enigmas to the end of their lives.

# CHAPTER X

## PRACTICAL COUNSELS

*" Prove all things : hold fast that which
is good."*—ST. PAUL.

*Be Practical.*—This is a weary commonplace,
but it happens to be a commonplace so important that we give it the *first* place. The
unpractical man is never successful in the
commercial sense; consequently, men who
are cast in the contemplative mould, or who
in other ways fail to see that life is action,
seldom obtain the standing-room they long
for in spite of themselves. " Temperament
is destiny." Speaking roughly, there
**Tempera-** are two classes of men: men of thought
**ment is** and men of action. We want the
**destiny.** thinkers and we want the workers; neither
class can be spared, for life is ideal as well
as real. But our point of view just now is
success in active pursuits, and the man who
brings into that sphere too much of the

contemplative spirit is destined to fail.  Whilst
he is *thinking,* the practical man is *acting;*
the one sacrifices chances of profit for the
sake of sentiment, the other has no ideal
sense to consult and pursues only what is
remunerative.  One could not wish to see a
more pitiable tragedy than that of a man,
who is by nature a student, engaged in
the business of trying to exist as a merchant.

Apart from temperament, however, it is
too evident that modern education has Defects in
a tendency to make men unpractical; education.
and this, in conjunction with a growing desire
to earn a " polite " living, is responsible for
many a sad failure.  " A very high education,
unless it is practical as well as classical and
scientific, too often unfits a man for contest
with his fellows: you have rifled the cannon
until the strength is gone.  Intellectual culture, if carried beyond a certain point, is
too often purchased at the expense of moral
vigour.  There is reason to fear that in the
case of not a few persons the mind is so
rounded and polished by education, so well
balanced, as not to be energetic in any one

faculty. They become so symmetrical as to have no point; while in other men not thus trained, the sense of deficiency, and of the sharp, jagged corners of their knowledge, lead to efforts to fill up the chasms, that render them at last far more learned and better educated men than the smooth, polished, easy-going graduate who has just knowledge enough to prevent the consciousness of his ignorance. . . . In short, the crown of all faculties **Men of thought and men of action.** is common sense. It is not the men of thought, but the men of action, who are best fitted to push their way to wealth and honour. The secret of all success lies in being alive to all that is going on around you; in adjusting one's self to its conditions; in being sympathetic and receptive; in knowing the wants of the time; in saying to one's fellows what they want to hear, or what they need to hear, at the right moment; in being the sum, the concretion, the result of the influences of the present time." [1] Shakespeare's Hamlet is the great dramatic type of the man who is called to action and is unable to respond. He loves learning and the joys of

[1] *Getting on in the World*, p. 138.

contemplation too much to enter the lists against his father's murderers. He can *think* with the best of his fellows; he can argue and be ˌhumorous, but *act* he cannot.   Doubtless this was the fault of Hamlet's temperament as much as his education, but no dramatic play has ever set forth with more relentless accuracy the piteous feebleness of intellectual strength minus the power of resolution.   Here is an illustration in the concrete.   " At a gathering in Australia not long since, four persons met, three of whom were shepherds on a sheep farm.   One of these had taken a degree at Oxford, another at Cambridge, the third at a German university.    The fourth was their employer, a squatter, rich in flocks and herds, but scarcely able to read and write, much less to keep accounts."   In analysing this picture two or three reflections stamp themselves indelibly on our minds.   The three men were highly educated, but it was not the education which has for its first aim the imparting of power to earn a living.   In that respect it is like a good deal of what passes as education in this country, but which is slowly yielding to

**Hamlet's "cursed spite."**

the utilitarian spirit.   Again, the three gradu-
ates are generally regarded as huge
failures.   In one sense they are, but
having settled down to farming and culti-
vated a love for it, they ought to do as
well if not better than the squatter himself.
What is to hinder them?   Only the lack of
practicality.

**Three
failures.**

What, then, more exactly, is meant by
practicality?   One writer thus answers the
question: "It is more easy to describe
by negatives than positives. . . . The
way in which a man acts in the minor relations of life, as a guest, as a host, as an
income-tax payer, or as a railway passenger,
decides whether he is a simpleton or world-
ling.   The former is perpetually coming to
grief.   If he is entertaining, he will abuse the
grandmother of the most influential man at
his table.   If he dines out, he will ask for fish
twice in spite of the waning proportions of
the cod.   As a contributor to the revenue he
is always in arrears, and incurring the terrors
of Somerset House. . . . In all dealings with
horseflesh he will be guided by the simple
rule of buying in the dearest market and

**Practicality
defined.**

selling in the cheapest. . . . To a subordinate
he will write with undue familiarity, or an air
of ridiculous assumption—to an equal with a
smack of arrogance."[1]   Now, these things are
characteristics of the unpractical man, but
they do not, after all, define practical talent
in its commercial aspect.  A talent for theory
is the power of *thinking;* a talent for **Thinking**
practice is the power of *doing;* hence, **and doing.**
practical talent is capacity for carrying business ideas into execution.   Let us take an
illustration.  Here are two men in business
as drapers; they are competitors in the same
city, and as yet have not succeeded in greatly
extending their borders.   The difference between them is primarily one of mental outlook.   One has never faced himself with the
question: "What am I in business for?" but
his competitor never asks himself any other
question, and as a result his custom is beginning to expand.   He is ready to confess that
he is in business to make money, consequently
his ideas are business ideas, and he **The spirit of**
has not the slightest intention of treat- **a bargain.**
ing his patrons philanthropically.  He is actu-

[1] *Getting on in the World*, p. 147.

ated after the manner of Shakespeare when he makes Hotspur say :—

> " I'll give thrice as much land to any well-deserving
>     friend,
> But in the way of bargain, mark you me,
> I'll cavil on the ninth part of a hair."

The other man is a routinist. He goes through the round of buying and selling, perhaps with considerable care, but he has not the right outlook. He will dress his window in such a way as to please his own taste rather than to give the best display; and in printing a catalogue he unconsciously sacrifices effectiveness to some æsthetic fad. He commits the sin of looking at business through his own eyes rather than the eyes of the public: in a word, he is too subjective. His competitor is always asking: "What do people want? How can I best display my goods? On what do I get the most profit?" There is not an atom of the subjective in him—when at business. His object is to deal with supply and demand, and many a time he laughs within himself at the crudities, inanities, and imbecilities of his customers, but what of that? He is not in

*Subjective v. objective.*

business to please himself or to act as critic
of other people's ways of spending money;
he exists to accumulate as much wealth as
possible in a speedy and legitimate manner.
If this ideal is not high enough for the
reader, then he had better turn his attention
elsewhere.

A false sense of modesty stands in the way
of some men who are otherwise keen    False
in their ambitions.    They know they    modesty.
have good things to sell, or that they are able
to score where their fellows fail, but they
shrink from the rough and tumble of competitive habits; they hesitate to advertise
themselves in the least degree, and pushful-
ness they abhor.   To a man of this type we
say: " *You must be an egoist.*"   So long as
you stick to the truth and stoop to no mean-
ness or positive wrong-doing, you need not
concern yourself with other people's feelings;
and you may be quite sure the other people
do not consider yours.   The world owes you
a living, and see that you get it.   Business
is not a sphere where altruism reigns    Be an egoist.
supreme and one trader politely refers his
customers to the shop opposite, where he is

sure " they will receive better stuff at less cost." A trader is in business for *himself,* not for the benefit of any one else, and the more selfish he is in the true sense, the better it will be for his half-yearly profits. He must be an egoist or—close his premises. Whatever call there is for self-sacrifice in the other departments of life, there is no call for it in commerce, which is avowedly founded on egoism, tempered by ethical feeling. Do not hesitate, then, to take off your coat and enter the arena. Put aside all silly bashfulness and foolish reserve, just as much as you would blatant egotism and vlugar " cheek," which is simply self-assertion without anything to assert. Sacrifice yourself for home and country, but never make a sacrifice in business unless it will be followed by advantageous results.

*Develop the power of initiative.*—To initiate is to begin, but the power of initiative means to begin, to continue, and to complete. Self-reliance is almost a synonymous term, but it carries with it a certain mistrustfulness from which the other phrase is free. To be self-reliant is still erroneously regarded

**Mistaken views.**

as a questionable virtue, and too nearly allied
with the vice of cocksureness.  Nothing could
be further from the truth.  Nevertheless, we
prefer to use the term at the head of this
section, because, whilst it advocates self-trust
in the highest degree, it makes no mention of
the " self," and deals with the subject from the
abstract point of view.  Life—at any rate
successful life, as we conceive it in these pages
—is *action,* and however clearly a man may
*think,* however skilfully he may draft the
details of a commercial campaign, if he cannot
*act* he might as well throw up the sponge, unless he can get others to act for him.  Initiative power is action plus mental ingenuity.

*Acquire the art of manipulating business
figures.*—The arithmetic of the schools forms
a good foundation for the kind of calculation
necessary in the world of business, but there
is still room for much improvement.  What
is wanted is not ability to work a great variety
of different sums, but the power to apply
figures to the facts of everyday life; and     "Sums"
*v.* business
time would be better spent in analysing     figures.
the formation of a table of commercial statistics

than by puzzling out wonderful questions about clocks or the speed of trains. The mental exercise of the former is quite as good as the latter, and is far more practical in its utility. Proficiency in business arithmetic requires (1) speed and accuracy of calculation, (2) an expert knowledge of bookkeeping, and (3) the faculty for applying figures to trade operations in ways not laid down in text-books.

**Three requisites.**

With reference to the first, little need be said: it is a matter of practice. At the same time, where buying and selling take place verbally, and prices are quoted and accepted, it is obviously important that calculations should be both rapid and correct, and very often the tardy man who trusts to approximate amounts finds to his chagrin that he is the loser. As far as possible every man should be his own ready-reckoner.

The second item calls for extended comment. There are few businesses where bookkeeping can be dispensed with, and although some men manage to rub along by using rule of thumb methods, they would probably do much better if they adopted a more scien-

**Bookkeeping in theory and practice.**

tific way of recording their transactions.
Bookkeeping as an academical subject is
now more intelligently taught than it used
to be, and it is possible to obtain a good working knowledge of the foundation principles
without even entering a counting-house. But,
after all, it is one thing to know the principles
and another thing to know how to use them.
This can only be learnt from experience. The
tendency of academical teaching is to elaborate;
the tendency of practical business is to simplify.
The bookkeeping of the college class-room is
an exact science; the bookkeeping of commerce
is an elastic adaptation of means to an end.
The business man should be an expert " not
merely in keeping accounts of payments and
receipts, of assets and liabilities, but also in
finding the results of his own special trading
by means of suitable systems of checking
constantly applied. By suitable systems are
meant such systems as, from their *simplicity*,
it is practicable to carry out. For it must be
remembered that, while too many business
men fail for want of keeping a sufficiently
comprehensive series of books, it is quite
possible to carry bookkeeping too far. It is

the discrimination which knows how far to go, and where to leave off, in this matter that distinguishes the bookkeeping of the schools from the bookkeeping of the trader."[1] The fact is that as competition increases profits can only be made to grow by effecting economies in the cost of production or in some other department of expenditure. To do this a merchant must

**Self-devised methods.** invent bookkeeping methods of his own, and it is here that we touch the third requisite of arithmetical proficiency, namely, the power to apply figures in an independent and original manner. The balance-sheet and the profit and loss account are a statement of *results* only; what the business man wants is the power to *analyse* those results by the introduction of other arithmetical processes.

For instance, here is a specimen taken from an actual business operation:—

[1] *Choosing a Calling and Making the Best of It.* By J. P. Collings.   P. 163.

| | Year ending Christmas 1880. | | Year ending Christmas 1881. | | Year ending Christmas 1882. | |
|---|---|---|---|---|---|---|
| Sales . . . . . . . | £18,520 | | £26,000 | | £36,600 | |
| Expenses. | £ | Percentage on Sales. | £ | Percentage on Sales. | £ | Percentage on Sales. |
| Wages . . . . . | 740 | 4.0 | 1120 | 4.3 | 1680 | 4.6 |
| Travellers (expenses, salaries, and commissions) . . . . | 780 | 4.2 | 1498 | 5.8 | 1568 | 4.3 |
| Rent, rates, gas, &c. . . | 480 | 2.6 | 604 | 2.3 | 760 | 2.1 |
| Interest on capital, 5% . | 200 | 1.1 | 260 | 1.0 | 365 | 1.0 |
| Carriage . . . . . . | 340 | 1.8 | 486 | 1.9 | 686 | 1.9 |
| Advertising . . . . . | 185 | 0.9 | 204 | 0.8 | 462 | 1.2 |
| Petty expenses . . . . | 140 | 0.8 | 284 | 1.1 | 201 | 0.5 |
| Allowance for bad debts, &c. . . . . . . | 260 | 1.4 | . 300 | 1.1 | 346 | 0.9 |
| | 3125 | 16.8 | 4756 | 18.3 | 6068 | 16.5 |
| Gross profit . . . . . | 3704 | 20.0 | 5331 | 20.5 | 7686 | 21.0 |
| Net profit . . . . . | 579 | 3.2 | 575 | 2.2 | 1618 | 4.7 |

" A summary such as this can scarcely fail to be a most valuable guide to traders in many lines of business. Of course the *form* of the summary may be altered to suit the nature and circumstances of different trades. A glance at the above particulars as they appear at the end of the year 1881 shows the trader in the first place that his *net* profit has *declined* from 3.2 per

**What a summary can teach.**

cent. to 2.2 per cent. Evidently something
is wrong. It now becomes necessary to discover where the weakness is. Have the
gross profits been too small, or the expenses
too high?

"A second glance at the summary shows the
trader that gross profits have actually increased from 20 per cent. to 20.5 per cent.,
but that his expenses have at the same time
increased from 16.8 per cent. to 18.3 per
cent. Clearly the weakness of his trading is
to be found in the increase in expenditure.

"His next anxiety is to discover where this
extra percentage of expenditure has crept in.
A further inspection of the figures gives him
the desired information. Evidently his ' petty
expenses' and ' travellers' salaries and com-
missions' are chiefly accountable for the
unsatisfactory state of things. It is clear
that he must keep his eye upon these items
during the coming year. Let us suppose
him to have done so, and that the 1882
stock-taking shows the results indicated in
the summary. The improvement is very
marked. Not only have the net profits re-
covered themselves, but they show an increase

on the year 1880.   This has been brought
about chiefly by watchfulness and improvement in respect to the two weak items mentioned above.

" Without some such information as the fore-
going to work upon, the trader is often led,
in the event of a bad stock-taking, to try and
recover his position by the wrong means.   For
instance, he *raises his prices* instead of *lowering
his expenses.*" [1]

But the power to apply figures in an independent and original manner is not confined
to bookkeeping processes; it takes in the
whole range of commercial activity.   For
instance, there is the power of estimat-
ing the possibilities of any particular
business in a particular place.   Given
a certain amount of data, and the shrewd
mathematician can calculate to a fairly approximate sum the likelihood of good remuneration.
In the higher walks of commerce, where large
undertakings and immense capital are involved,
the safety of every important movement is
necessarily guarded by careful investigations
into figures; and in life assurance corpora-

The power of
the mathe-
matician.

[1] *Choosing a Profession*, p. 183.

K

tions the actuary is really the most important officer: in other words, the vast business done by these colossal companies has been based on the skill of the mathematician. It is a fact not without significance that Mr. Pierpont Morgan won considerable fame in all branches of mathematics whilst a student at Göttingen. One might almost go so far as to say that no man can hope to achieve distinctive success who has no " head for figures."

*Be a Specialist.*—The word is one with strong medical associations. The general practitioner is set over against the specialist who has devoted years of study to some particular organ of the body, *e.g.* the heart. He may be full of inward hesitation in the treatment of common ailments, but if he knows

**Specialism in medicine.** one thing well, that hesitation is no discredit to him. The time spent in one specific direction, to the benefit of thousands of sufferers, is time spent in the service of humanity, and the loss in breadth of knowledge is more than compensated for in depth of insight.

The same holds good in law. Barristers

and solicitors take up special departments;
one company law, another the law of patents,
and another municipal law. The reason for
this course is quite plain. The realm of
knowledge has become so great and so wide,
that no man can hope to master the whole of
it; he must take a portion of it and be content to know that alone.

Of late years business affairs have shown
a tendency to follow the lines of special- **In business.**
ism. Competition has produced a demand
for excellence which cannot be met without
the employment of the best brains and the
highest skill; and some businesses are so
large and composite in character that it is
necessary to engage men for exclusive attention to one department. There is a further
tendency for like businesses of small size to
amalgamate together, and this again is another
argument in favour of the specialist. The
first duty in the science of life is to know all
about the details of the calling which takes
up the major part of our time. There is no
room now for the " jack of all trades," **No more**
and the man with hobbies is finding **"jacks."**
it necessary to curtail the hours he used

to spend upon them.  In the old days, when there were fewer people to compete with, and life was a slower thing, men could afford to be leisurely, and allow a generous margin for recreation; they could even afford to turn out work that was not of the very best.  Those days are gone.  Competition is not a fancy skirmish with pop-guns, it is a fight to a finish; and the man who is an authority upon one thing is of more service than the man who knows everything.  " The day of the all-round man is over.  New conditions have come into business life, and they have come to stay.  Nobody wants the all-round man, nobody cares for his particular kind of ability.  Industries have been rearranged.  They are now separated into departments instead of plants.  At the head of each of these departments is wanted a man who knows all about a particular division, who has concentrated his entire mind and ability to its requirements and possibilities, who is, in fact, a highly trained, highly

The day of developed specialist.  Men like these
the expert. are scarce to-day.  Hundreds of institutions are looking for them.  Salaries ranging

from $5000 to $15,000 are waiting for them.
My own concern is looking for half-a-dozen
specialists to-day, rubber men, lumber men,
&c. We would cheerfully pay them $5000
a year, and even more cheerfully $15,000;
for a $15,000 man is a great deal more valu-
able to his concern than the $5000 man. But
he has got to be a $15,000 man. Naturally he
is not plentiful." [1]

What is true in America is quickly becom-
ing true here in England. To meet these
changing conditions every man should have
his speciality, otherwise he will find himself
left behind. True, there are certain occupations to which the specialist doctrine would
seem to have little or no relation; they are
not divided up into departments, and many of
them are most profitable when run on small
and individual lines. But even then the man
who knows his business better than his
fellows enjoys a great advantage over them.
They are content with the average; he is
content with nothing short of the superlative,
and experience proves that the superlative

[1] C. R. Flint, President of the U. S. Rubber Co., in the
*Saturday Evening Post.*

means money where the average only equals a bare living.

No; the specialist is the coming man. If a soldier, he will be like Napoleon, who could make powder if he wanted it, or gun-carriage wheels if one should break down. Nothing about war is strange to the ideal defender of his country. If a tea merchant, he will do more than buy cheap and sell dear—when he can; he will know the nature of the tea-growing soils, the effects of various kinds of water in the brewing of the beverage, and by experiments become highly proficient in the evolving of skilful mixtures and new flavours. Expert knowledge carries with it an increasing premium of money value, and those who, to use the common phrase, mean to " get on," should see to it that they adapt their line of action in accordance with this fact.

But the specialist has more to say for himself than that he is likely to make more money than the all-round man: he can claim more respect in the eyes of the world as an educated man in the commercial sense of the term. Let us suppose that his speci-

*The coming man.*

*His apologia.*

ality lies in knowing how, when, and where to buy silks. The all-round man understands a little about silk goods, and also a little about cotton goods; he has dabbled with wools and linens, and is not quite a stranger to West of England fabrics; in fact, he has a working knowledge of these products. Now, which of these two men—perhaps equally estimable in character—has the higher status? The specialist of course. He knows things generally, but on one thing he is an authority—a subject on which his opinion is sought, and which, when given, claims the respect due to an expert. Mediocrity, says La Bruyère, is unendurable in art. It will soon be unendurable in business.

*If you are in a salaried position, learn the duties of the man above you.*—This sounds very simple and very obvious, and yet it is a suggestion that the Englishman is slow to act upon. He has a strong feeling that it is best to do his own work well and wait for a promotion. New duties can be learned afterwards. Besides, he is prepared to argue that it is impossible to learn the duties of the man above you; that it

English conservatism.

is impertinent to attempt to do so; and that the effort is calculated to defeat its own ends.

We are afraid his arguments cannot be sustained. There is no need to thrust yourself unpleasantly into another man's sphere, and blatantly demand that he shall show you how his work is done. Observation and a little tact is all that is required. No two positions in an office or factory are so utterly separated that the affairs of one have no connection with those of another: a business is an organism, and each department is, or should be, a vital part of the whole. Hence, opportunities to know the mysteries of work, other than that you are engaged in, will inevitably present themselves; and by dint of a quick eye and a little deft questioning, the duties of

**How other duties are "learned."** the man above you become an open book. The advantage of such knowledge is, of course, considerable. When the man above you falls ill suddenly, and some one is required to take his place, the business manager is glad to avail himself of a competent junior, and he does not forget the fact when the time for promotion comes round.

The English policy of "minding one's own business" is sane enough; but there are some things that are sane without being progressive, and this disinclination to meddle with another employee's duties is one of them.

*Cultivate a sense of humour.*—Is this superfluous counsel? Not at all. There are many men and women who need no advice in this direction, but there are many who do. They take life very seriously, very literally, and whilst other people see "points" and scream with laughter, the phlegmatic folks either stamp with vexation or suffer deep but unnecessary humiliation of spirit. To these we offer a word of counsel. There is enough sorrow, trouble, deceit, and infamy in the world to make the angels weep; and if we care to investigate the conduct of business behind the scenes, there is enough to shatter all belief in man as an image of God, and to confirm the dogma of total depravity. But is there nothing else in the world? and is there not a time to laugh as well as **Heraclitus and Democritus.** to weep? We are not called upon to follow Heraclitus, the weeping philosopher, on the one hand, or Democritus, the laughing philosopher, on the other hand. It is difficult to say which is the worse type of the two; the man who is always snivelling about human sorrow, or the man who idiotically giggles at everything.

The mission of humour is to restore the balance which has been lost to us by the toil and bitterness of life—at any rate, that is its first office. "A man who is easily disheartened does not appear to be destined by nature for the overcoming of difficulties, and nothing is a happier incentive to the maintenance of good animal spirits than the quick sense of humour which finds something to make a jest of even in conditions which bring but a sinking of the heart to the less fortunately endowed mortal. One can hardly read the story of any escape from shipwreck, any drifting about in an open boat over wintry seas, without learning of some plucky and humorous mortal who kept his comrades alive and alert through all dangers and troubles by his ready humour and animal spirits. Read any account of a long protracted siege, when the besieged had to resist assault from

**Laughter and resolution.**

without and hunger within, and you will be sure to be told how the humorous sallies of some leader were able to prevent those around him from sinking into the depths of despair. There are times when no good whatever is done by taking even the most serious things too seriously." [1]

Men who have made up their minds to succeed, or die in the attempt, should remember the last sentence. To take serious things too seriously generally means the lunatic asylum. There are plenty of serious things in the life of the would-be successful man, and if he has a saving sense of humour he will often keep afloat when his less endowed neighbour goes under. Did not Mark Twain lose all his money and joke his way back again to competency? Yes; it will be retorted, he was a humorist, and could never be killed by trouble. It would be nearer the truth to say he was a man of iron will, with a fine sense of honour and an appreciation of the humorous. As a rule the great humorist has a keen sense of melancholy. When Carlini was convulsing

**Taking things too seriously.**

[1] Justin H. M'Carthy.

Naples with laughter, a patient waited on a physician in that city to obtain some remedy **Carlini.** for excessive melancholy which was rapidly consuming his life. The physician endeavoured to cheer his spirits, and advised him to go to the theatre and hear Carlini. He replied, " I am Carlini."

The question is not one of natural optimism or pessimism; it is the simpler matter of being able to see the funny side of grave things. Something depends on a native gift, but something also depends on cultivation. In reading the biographies of men of mark one notices that for the most part they were determined to be cheerful. Their first defeat was a keen **Be cheerful.** experience, but the second, though quite as keen, took less energy out of them, and, in spite of severe loss, they continued work with undiminished vigour. The value of such power to adjust mental conditions is exceedingly great; in fact, it often makes all the difference between radiant hope and black despair.

*Remember the value of tact.*—It has been said that talent is something, but tact is everything. The saying easily lends itself to criticism; it is clumsy and cynically empty of the quality it describes, and yet it contains a good deal of truth.   There is a sense in which tact *is* everything, simply because it is a **Tact is** course of action that varies in a thou- **everything.** sand ways with a thousand different circumstances.   Tact is essentially the art of adjusting the relationships between ourselves and others; and as these relationships are almost infinite in number and character, it is evident that the absence of ability to adjust them with satisfaction to ourselves, and without injustice to others, is a serious disqualification in the struggle for success.

Take the question of clothes.   A well-dressed man, silk - hatted, frock - coated, and with shiny boots, may be a saint or a **Clothes.** diabolical sinner; but when we meet him for the first time, his presentable appearance, rightly or wrongly, means more to us than if he were clad carelessly in fustian and wore a stubbly beard of two days' growth.   We know that a worthy man may be clothed in rags, but if he is, one of two things must speedily happen—the rags will go or else his worthiness will be shortlived.   There is too much cant on this question of dress.   Literal people,

persuaded that dress is nothing and soul everything, are accustomed to say, when referring
to a badly-dressed man, " A man's a man for
a' that." They say it as if it were a fact discovered by themselves, and they ventilate it
Moral merit   so freely that one almost comes to be-
in trousers.   lieve there is moral merit in trousers
that bag at the knees, and shoes that are down
at the heel, and hats that show the signs of
many a storm.

The matter is really a very simple one.   In
the abstract, good clothes, bad clothes, indifferent clothes mean nothing at all.   Clothes
are merely a covering for the body, the man
himself is the chief thing.   But in the concrete of daily life we see clothes first and
character afterwards.   We observe that people
judge much by appearances in spite of fre-
quent deception, and it is borne in upon us
that in many commercial circles the wearing
Silk-hat   of an uncomfortable silk-hat is the hall-
philosophy.   mark of acceptability.   We may demur
as much as we please; we may even dare to
confront a great financier by wearing a hard
felt bowler, but we cannot abolish the facts as
we find them.   Now it is here where the

tactician comes in. He believes, possibly, that dress is nothing and soul everything, and yet he believes just strongly in the law of adjustment. If he finds that a few extra suits of clothes a year mean more business, he buys them without a murmur; if there is some subtle connection between the glossy silk of a new hat and the incoming of larger orders, he will not begrudge a guinea now and again; in a word, he is a man of tact who is prepared to adapt himself to the types of humanity by which he is surrounded.

This adaptation takes another form; it suggests the government of speech. **Tact in** There is a time to speak and a time to **speech.** be silent, and the business man with diplomatic instincts knows these times to a nicety. He does not blurt out information about his own affairs, either spontaneously or when being " pumped " by a cunning adversary; he knows the value of a secret, even a small one, and agrees to take seriously what is frequently considered as a triviality. For this same reason he places high value on the information others blurt out about themselves, and his ears are always ready to listen to anything that is not empty gossip. There is a curious notion abroad that the exercise of any repression in speech denotes a weak man, and that the strong man is an individual with peculiar emphasis, who glories in calling "a spade a spade." No such thing. "Tact," says Mr.

**Mr. Lecky speaks.** Lecky, "is not merely shown in saying the right thing at the right time, and to the right people; it is shown quite as much in many things that are left unsaid or only lightly or evasively touched."[1] A weak man will call another man a liar on insufficient evidence; a strong man restrains his speech and keeps a customer.

This question of using conversation tactfully is a very important one for business men who are aiming at success. In buying and selling, how much depends on the power of putting things! La Bruyère, with his accustomed insight, aptly remarks that "it is a misfortune not to be able to speak well, nor to have sense enough to hold one's tongue." That is the whole matter in a nutshell. Ability to express one's self clearly, to argue forcibly, to arrange facts in their proper order,

[1] *The Map of Life*, p. 322.

and press a conclusion home—this power is
not required in the pulpit, and at the bar, or on
the political platform alone; it is required in
most branches of trade, and is a great advantage in every walk of life. Elocution for   **Commercial**
commercial purposes is an idea that   **elocution.**
may sound a trifle absurd, but if a few lessons
would change the mumble - jumble of many
business conversations into something like
coherency, it would be better for business
despatch, and certainly better for the chances
of success.

In earlier days what is called the line of least
resistance had not much popularity; when a
man had a difficulty with another he took the
line of greatest resistance and declared war to
the knife. In these days we are more   **Tact in**
ready to believe in diplomacy, not because   **diplomacy.**
we are more spiritually-minded, but because
diplomacy is generally cheaper in the long
run. Rather than endure the expense and
publicity of a trial in the courts, we prefer to
submit to an arbitration, or settle difficulties
ourselves on the principle of " give and take."
The motive may not be love of brotherhood,
but if it results in the multiplying of more

peaceable relations, and the conserving of capital, the nature of the motive may be allowed to pass.

Lastly, the tactician is a man of manners.

**Manners.** There still lingers among us the notion that a loud and boisterous style is the only one that is impressive and effective in the conduct of business. The sole justification for this erroneous conception is that life on the competitive plane tends to develop selfishness, and selfishness means egoism, and egoism means rudeness. But does it? Not necessarily. A man who runs in a race is a great egoist. He does not care a straw about the others, and he wants no one of them to win; in fact, he spent months of severe training with the express object of winning the race himself, and he will be very disappointed if he is not the first at the goal. But, although he is such an egoist, it is possible for him to be a perfect gentleman and a man of spotless honour. He need stoop to no trickery, bribery, or unfair means of attaining his ends, and he can treat other competitors with the utmost courtesy without diminishing his own efforts to succeed in the contest.

It is the same in commercial relationships. Success in business is a race between rivals, but rivalry need not engender bad manners. The rude, vulgar, swear-and-tear kind of man may attract attention, but in the long run brains and diplomacy win the race. Courtesy is not a dear article, and as an investment it pays brilliantly. What is more, everybody knows its value. Even the uncouth "that-is-my-price-and-if-you-don't-like-it-you-may-go-to-the-devil" kind of man appreciates a delicate compliment or a small attention.

**Honour in rivalry.**

It will be urged at this juncture that the mannerly man is frequently an effeminate man. *Sometimes,* not *frequently.* But what of that? A mannerly man can say and write disagreeable things quite as easily and forcefully as the man who does nothing else. If a traveller has returned from a journey without a single order, palpably due to carelessness, is a proprietor any the less mannerly because he takes the delinquent "drummer" to task, and in severe tones assures him that another such journey will mean instant dismissal? To administer reproofs in loud,

**Politeness and effeminacy.**

bawling language, accompanied by wealth of curse and gesticulation, is accounted a proper thing in some circles, but this line of action seldom accomplishes its object, and, besides, it is unspeakably vulgar.   There is far more effeminacy in these hysterical ravings than in the sober chastisement which clothes itself in few words.   Subordinates get accustomed to the governor's " fits," and say, " He can't help it," or " He'll be all right in the morning."   But if a new governor comes who *says* little but *acts* more, these same subordinates soon take their man's measure; so that when he says, " I'm annoyed," it means quite as much as if he threw the ledgers about the office, and made the atmosphere blue with his sulphureous language.

**The weak and the strong.**

The relations between employer and employed are only a section of life in which manners play a part.   There is the customer to consider.   He is a strangely compounded person: parts are good, some are bad, others are indifferent.   Then how whimsical he is— or she!   You follow instructions faithfully, to find them cancelled at the last moment; and when you expostulate mildly you get a curt letter asking your traveller not to call again. The customer often deals carelessly with accounts. You wait for your money, and then write for it, only to find that the account has been "lost" and asking for another copy. Yes, the customer is a trying person, whether he buys by the thousand-pound cheque or the penny piece. The question is: Can we be polite to him? Well, try the other way and see. You will soon conclude that the polite way is the only way. After all the customer is not half-bad when you get to know him; in fact he is rather like yourself: he wants good value for his money, and he appreciates a cheerful manner. You must make up your mind to give the public better treatment than you think it deserves. The public is often given to insults; sometimes it will deliver them by word of mouth, sometimes act them by flourishing a competitor's goods in your face. But take the advice of a professor who said to his students: "Young gentlemen, have two pockets made—a large one to hold the insults and a small one to hold the fees." Perhaps the professor exaggerated the question of

*Customer and tactful handling.*

*How to deal with insults.*

insult, but at any rate the world of business is full of trying elements, and the man who can unite the tact of etiquette with the other factors of success, is in possession of a power the helpful influence of which it is difficult to over-estimate.

# CHAPTER XI

## CONCLUSION

WE have now completed the programme set out at the beginning, and may profitably devote a little space to final reflections. We have endeavoured to treat the subject of success on inductive lines by considering man and his powers in relation to surrounding circumstance. Our findings have been distinctly hopeful. It is plain that to a man of health and average ability success is not a tantalising mirage **Hope for the** in a desert of expired opportunities; it **average man.** is a substantial reality which is faithful to all its promises. The key to progress is originality, and the key to originality in business is vital interest. Let a man be as enthusiastic in his business as he is in his pleasures, and the day of enlargement will soon begin to dawn. True, there are powers over which he exercises no control, and which act upon him, and upon all others, with apparent purposelessness; but, as these powers of fate and fortune are beyond his ken, it is his duty to leave them **Luck.** out of the reckoning, and work on as if they did not exist. If they should favour him, let him be thankful; if not, then, even though it be impossible to receive the stroke in Christian resignation, he can submit with pagan stoicism. We saw, however, that, in a large measure, success was essentially a human product, and the direct fruit of human endeavour, having little to do with agencies lying outside the area of buying and selling. The real limitations lie in ourselves, not in "luck." We can never say "all things are possible," or "all men can be successful" in the material sense; but we *can* say that after the last analysis the real obstacles are few.

Gathering together the lessons of the preceding chapters, we are inclined to state them **Lessons learned.** in the following manner:—

(i.) Luck is comparatively a minor matter.

(ii.) There is still plenty of scope for the man of average ability.

(iii.) The prime requisite is force, energy.

Luck is a minor matter because we know practically nothing of its operations. The man who waits for its coming generally has to wait a long time, and is frequently disappointed with the result. On the other hand, the man who does not wait at all is more often the favourite of fortune; and, if there be any traceable method in the luck of opportunities, it is that they have a tendency to cluster in those quarters where merit is supreme.

The second point is much more important. We have sufficiently indicated the immense advantage of physical health, mental power, and superior education, in conjunction with good character; and shall not be misunderstood when we say that the day of the average man has not gone by. But it must be an average that grows. Average ability may begin the way to success; it ceases to be average long before the end is reached. The process employed is the education **Education by** of experience — precisely the kind of **experience.** ability that one never gets from books. What book can teach the art of judgment and decision? A book can expound the theory of life, and even supply fruitful suggestions as to its practice; but the actual thing must be lived to know it.

Every youth of average ability, reading the story of commercial achievements, is not so often inspired as may be imagined; he is frequently depressed with the thought that his powers are too slender to accomplish anything half so distinctive. We congratulate him on his modesty, and the good sense he shows in moderating his ambitions and in not overrating himself. But his depression should give way to hope, for hope is well founded if ordinary intelligence has force behind it. This brings us to the third point—the most

**Force and energy.** important of all. Difference in mental power, pure and simple, does not matter a great deal in reference to our particular subject; it is force that makes the difference between men. Where force is united to uncommon ability, we have the great man of whom Emerson speaks. In modern times Bismarck was a good specimen of the type; whereas Kant's transcendent powers were of little political consequence because he lacked personal and aggressive force. It is the same in business. Capacity for action in some form is an absolute necessity. A man may design a very wonderful machine, but if he can't evolve steam to set the wheels agoing, he must give place to the man who can. Metaphorically speaking, the basic difference between man and man is the power of generating steam. England's competitors are not a bit cleverer than her own sons, but they have more force, and they naturally forge ahead.

Now the secret of force is vital interest in work. Let a man love his work, and there are few limits we can set him. He **Vital interest** may become one-sided, a little dense to **once more.** idealism, and too " shoppy " in his conversation, but in his business he will be a prince, although he started as a man of average ability. On a previous page we stated that if this type of character did not commend itself to the reader's taste he had better turn elsewhere. He is not to be blamed if temperament leads him away from competitive strife, and suggests a snug clerkship, or a post where the hours of labour leave sufficient margin for some study or pastime; but he

must not blame the constitution of the world
**Temperament again.** if his school friends, by narrowing down
their 'energies, achieve considerable for-
tune whilst he remains a poor man. Why
should he sneer at wealth when all the time
he covets it; and why should he expect to
prosper when his deepest interest lies not
in work, but hobbies? There are more ideals
in life than one—fortunately—and the man
who is true to his own best instincts is a
good man anywhere, whether success has
been purchased at the cost of culture, or
culture at the cost of success—in the material
sense. A certain unfriendliness will always
exist between the varied temperaments, and
just as St. Peter—the man of action—was
impatient with St. John—the man of thought
—witness the former's sarcastic question:
"What shall this man do?"—so will the man
of force to-day extend his pity to the poor
individual who can spend his evenings studying the poetry of Dante. Perhaps the time
will come when we shall understand each
other better, but at present it is a long way
off.

But for success there is small chance for the

man of contemplative mould: it is, first, action; second, action; third, action; and action **Action to** to the very last. A man must have some **the end.** natural force in him, and he must also be capable of an absorbing interest. Only then will his full powers be called into activity, and out of this activity, continuously exercised, will spring the glory of an accomplished work.

And when success has been won! what follows? Happiness? That depends on the man. Misers are generally sup- **Happiness?** posed to be miserable, but many of them evolve a tolerable satisfaction out of their hoarded gains. The current moralising of the day speaks consolingly of the utter wretchedness there is in possessing vast sums of money, but even moralists seldom refuse legacies. There is a good deal of cant abroad about money and happiness. On the one hand, we have poor people who talk poetically of love in a cottage, and the vice of being vulgarly rich, when all the time they are coveting a pleasant villa not far away, and an income to enable them to live in it; on the other hand, we have the wealthier classes who affect desires for a simpler life and fewer wants, when, in their hearts, they envy everybody wealthier than themselves.

The fact is, success, in the sense of getting money, will not of itself bring happiness if the man has any idealism in his soul; but if his nature is metallic, there is no reason in the world why his satisfaction should not be complete. The happiness of the successful man is really a question for himself to decide. He knows better than we do whether he has dwarfed his nature and starved his mind, or whether his real pleasures are now to begin by dispensing wealth to those who need it most.

It depends on the man.

Of course there are events in every life with which mere money has nothing to do. If a rich man loses his only son, and never recovers from the loss, why begin to moralise and say: " With all his money he is not happy "? Would a poor man be any the happier? " Happiness by money " is after all very absurd, for there are so many conditions necessary to secure so great a blessing, and money is only one of them. Health, surely, takes a prior place to riches.

Money and bereavements.

In this sense, therefore, the struggle for a place that ends in failure may have elements of happiness that are partial compensation; but for all our readers we sincerely hope and trust theirs will be the struggle that ends in success.

**The last wish.**

THE END

www.ingramcontent.com/pod-product-compliance
Lightning Source LLC
Chambersburg PA
CBHW081229090426
42738CB00016B/3232